A Double Spring

A Double Spring

A year of tragedy, grief and love

JULIET DARLING

ALLEN&UNWIN

SYDNEY · MELBOURNE · AUCKLAND · LONDON

First published in 2013

Copyright © Juliet Darling 2013

Allen & Unwin
83 Alexander Street
Crows Nest NSW 2065
Australia
Phone: (61 2) 8425 0100
Fax: (61 2) 9906 2218
Email: info@allenandunwin.com
Web: www.allenandunwin.com

Cataloguing-in-Publication details are available
from the National Library of Australia
www.trove.nla.gov.au

ISBN 978 1 74331 505 7

Internal design by Kirby Armstrong
Illustration by Torey Wahlstrom
Set in 11/15 pt Sabon Pro by Bookhouse, Sydney
Printed and bound in Australia by Griffin Press

10 9 8 7 6 5 4 3 2 1

MIX
Paper from
responsible sources
FSC
www.fsc.org FSC® C009448

The paper in this book is FSC® certified.
FSC® promotes environmentally responsible,
socially beneficial and economically viable
management of the world's forests.

For Nick

Preface

Nick Waterlow OAM was born in Hitchin, UK, in 1941. He was one of the first international independent art curators. His work as the director of three Sydney Biennales helped the Biennale become an international showcase for contemporary art.

He held many key positions in the Sydney art world, and was for twenty years the director of the Ivan Dougherty Gallery, College of Fine Arts (COFA), University of New South Wales, where he curated and oversaw many original and thought-provoking exhibitions.

While Nick's passion was for contemporary art he was sustained by great art from all eras, and in all fields. He could discard the trivial and the mediocre, glide over the inessentials and, with his discerning eye, look for 'the good of what is made'. He held no creed: he was open and sceptical and when he was critical of art it was always for the sake of truth.

Nick's empathetic nature allowed him to engage with all kinds of people, and with a tireless curiosity and interest he brought out the best in others. He loved art. And he was that rarest of human beings, he loved artists, and he was utterly devoted to their calling.

I am an artist. Nick and I met in 1998. We lived together with my son for ten years. This book celebrates our free and precious friendship and love. But while our love and world were expanding, something sinister and hidden was gathering with a momentous force.

Nick had three children with his first partner, and his eldest son Antony suffered from schizophrenia. Antony was never scheduled or treated for his illness. There were all manner of warnings and forebodings but no one was able to interpret them or stop the intractable course of events, until the evening of 9 November 2009 when, in a frenzied knife attack, Antony killed his father and sister.

This book is my perspective of what it was like to live in the shadow of an impending death; with the weight of the tragedy and the bitterness of grief. It also honours the acts of charity and grace that arose from it. Ultimately, it is a story of love.

Juliet Darling
Sydney

Contents

PART THREE

PART FOUR

PART FIVE

But the monstrosities and the murderous days,
How do you endure them, how do you take them?—I praise.

Rainer Maria Rilke

There was no shortage of red flags that indicated he had a problem, but Antony was able to manipulate the process. The doctors found nothing to say he was at 'immediate risk'. The family saw something wrong with him, and were exposed to his unstable behaviours, but in front of doctors Antony was able to present himself, to deceive. The doctors were not able to schedule him against his will.

There will be questions that we will never answer. Where he went for those eighteen days we'll never know. It is one of those little blanks in the story. We'll get by without it. They are not that important to the events.

Homicide Detective
27 March 2012

PART ONE

I heard the news

It was a little after ten-thirty on a spring night. Nick had not arrived home from his visit to his daughter Chloe's house but I was expecting him to walk in at any minute. I was in bed reading when I heard the phone. I sat up, leant forward and held my breath to listen to the voice on the answering machine in the hallway. My heart stiffened. I recognised Nick's younger son's voice, and I jumped up and ran through the darkness to grab the receiver.

'There's something on the internet,' Luke said.

'What?' I could hear him tapping the keys on a computer. 'What is it?'

'I'll bring it up.' He was still tapping the keys.

'Tell me. Just tell me.'

'Two bodies have been found in Randwick.'

'Two bodies? That means they're dead! That means Antony has finally done it!'

'Er, yeah,' said Luke.

'Yeah? What do you mean "yeah"?'

3

'Where are you?'

'At home.'

'The police are arriving now. They're at the door.'

'Can I talk to them? Put them on.' I heard myself crying: No, no, no, no.

There was a pause, then I heard a woman's voice in the background. Then she came on the phone. 'I'm a friend of Luke's. Just stay calm. Calm down.'

'Put the police on. I want to talk to them.'

'They can't talk to you on the phone. Stay there. They're going to come to you afterwards.' She hung up.

I walked into the bedroom and put on some clothes. I made myself a hot-water bottle and sat motionless with the shadows moving soundlessly across the walls, my heart pounding in my chest and the blood moving slowly through my veins—in that room where Nick and I used to love one another among the shadows of the swaying branches. I closed the curtains and then I sat and stared at the geometric pattern on the Persian carpet.

At one-thirty am the intercom buzzed. I picked up the receiver. A male voice said, 'It's the police.' I let them in then opened the front door and waited for them to climb the stairs.

The police had been here before, five years ago, looking for Antony, who had used our address on his driver's licence. They hadn't believed me when I told them that Antony didn't live here. I thought they had come to tell me that Nick had been murdered then, but apparently Antony had smashed up a backpackers' hostel in Bondi and had been captured on video.

This time, two policemen in uniform entered our apartment. One of them said, 'The bodies of a middle-aged woman and an elderly man have been found.'

'Who?'

'We don't have any names.'

'Nick Waterlow? Chloe?'

They didn't respond. They had come to tell me something they couldn't tell me. But I already knew. My body told me. As I moved forward to close the door, suddenly I had to double over, and as I stood in the bright light of the doorway, which at that moment seemed to represent all of space, I felt something enter my being. A rush of warmth that came up from the ground and moved through my feet and rose up through my body to my head. I stood fixed in that position, bent over my feet, for what seemed an eternity, but it couldn't have been very long because the policemen were still in the hall watching me, and they hadn't come to my assistance—and they hadn't said anything. At last I pulled myself up, and slowly, mechanically followed them into the living room. The policemen sat together on the sofa. I noticed a small rubber ball on the carpet. I felt the need to pick it up. I bent over and with both hands took hold of it; it felt like lead, and I struggled to lift it onto the piano. I could feel the steady gaze of the policemen, and I saw one of them glance at our old cedar clock on the bookshelf; it had stopped at eight o'clock years ago and I had never bothered to repair it.

I was experiencing time in a different way. Time was no longer something I could measure with a dial on the face of a clock; it was bigger but I could measure it with my heart. I was outside of it all—yet I was inside an eternal present.

I turned on the standard lamp and we sat in silence for a long while facing one another. They didn't say anything and nor did I.

I was thinking about their words, 'an elderly man'. I have never thought of Nick as that. 'If only you knew how young he was,' I thought, almost with contempt.

When I met Nick he was bald, with white hair combed at the back; his body was slightly collapsed and the folds of his skin hung loosely off his limbs. Still, I thought he was so young, and as open and innocent as a child—and as wise. The fact that he carried his delightful childlike innocence well into his maturity was what first attracted me to him.

At last one of the policemen said, 'We've been to see Luke. When we told him what had happened he behaved very strangely.'

'What did he do?'

'We're not at liberty to tell you that.'

I was lost in a dream. The police had arrived to tell me something they couldn't tell me but they knew that I knew. And I didn't care that they couldn't answer my questions. I knew all I needed to know.

I thought about Luke, and how he might have behaved. Was he indifferent? Did he laugh? Maybe he was relieved. Maybe he felt nothing, nothing at all.

I was wondering if I should stay that night in the apartment alone.

'Am I safe here?'

'Yes. Antony would be mad to come by here,' one of them said.

I let them out, and returned to the living room, where I walked around in a circle. 'But Antony is mad,' I thought. I tried to ring my son George but he didn't answer. I sent him a text. He was asleep or his phone was off. I sent my friend Jane Campion a text. *Call me. It's about Nick.* She didn't reply either. I rang my sister Camilla in Cairns. Her husband Jamie answered.

'Nick has been murdered by his son. He's dead.'

'What?'

I heard him calling to Camilla, trying to wake her. Camilla came to the phone.

'Stay on the line. Don't hang up,' she said. 'I'm calling Fiona on the mobile.'

There was a pause while she called our friend, Fiona Waller. Then she was back.

'Fiona will pick you up. Pack a few things. She'll take you to her place.'

I threw some clothes in a bag, and I waited by the door. When the buzzer rang I went down to the street. A black sedan was stopped in the middle of the road, with the engine idling and its high beam flashing. Fiona's son Sam, whom I hadn't seen since he was ten, was now a six-foot, well-built twenty-one-year-old. He was standing in the middle of the road with a golf driver in his hand. Fiona was in the back seat. I got in and she grabbed me and held me tight as Sam drove us very carefully through the empty dark streets to their home in a nearby suburb.

Fiona gave me a sleeping pill, and I fell asleep, sitting up, in their daughter's bed with the light on. Fiona's husband Craig saw the light when he went to the bathroom. He didn't turn it off, he told me the next day, because the switch was on the wall, and he would have had to lean over me to reach it—he didn't want to frighten me.

•

After the longest night I woke early to the singing of their eleven-year-old, who was doing her homework in the hall. I got up to walk down the road to Ross Mellick and Margaret Raffan's house. They are both dear friends of Nick's.

'I'm looking forward to cutting down the workload and spending more time with good friends like Ross,' Nick had said recently.

'Ross loves me,' I told Nick playfully.

'He loves me more,' said Nick.

I walked down the street as if sleepwalking, under the jacarandas in bloom. I knocked on the garden gate, which was locked as usual. There was no bell, so I called out over the fence. It was six o'clock but I knew they both rose early. Then I saw Margaret, with her dog on a leash, walking up the street towards me.

'Juliet! What are you doing here?'

I told her. She didn't say anything, just motioned for me to follow her into the house. She went to the bathroom and Ross came out with a towel around his waist and he hugged me tight.

•

Two homicide detectives arranged to meet me at our apartment that afternoon. My friend Lisa Hochhauser had flown down from Byron Bay, and she was standing in the street outside the building waiting for me to arrive. We went inside and the young detectives sat side by side at the table, at the place where Nick used to sit and work each night after dinner. They wore matching grey suits, and their mobiles were placed in front of them, on the table. Every few minutes their phones would ring, one phone and then the other, and both mobiles had the same ringtone.

I stopped still. 'What is it?'

'*The Godfather*,' said Lisa.

'Is it? I'm not sure. Maybe not.'

'It's *The Sopranos*.'

'I think it might be.'

'No, it's *The Godfather*.'

Lisa and I began to laugh, and soon we were laughing hysterically. The detectives didn't say anything, they sat at the table, not moving a muscle, watching us. Just like in the movies.

After Lisa and I calmed down, one of them turned to me. 'Did Nick have any enemies?'

I flashed to one of the homicide police shows on television. I had seen this scene numerous times. This was a crime show but, as my son described it when he was little, it was in 'the real air'.

I thought about the word 'enemy'. So many people loved Nick. But of course, he must have had detractors. But who? There was the man from the university who had asked me at the Bacchus Ball whether Nick had any plans to retire. But that did not make him an enemy. Nick didn't think badly of anyone; I'd never heard him speak negatively of anyone, not once. A hundred different faces appeared before my eyes, each one a friend. There were his children. Can a child be an enemy? Yes. His son Antony was an enemy.

'No, he didn't have enemies. I really believe Antony has killed Nick and Chloe,' I said.

'It couldn't have been someone else?'

Perhaps they believed Antony hadn't done it. I wasn't about to read the papers but I knew that the story was on the front page and that the police were looking for him. Did they think I had done it? These homicide detectives weren't going to presume anything. One of them asked me if I knew how Antony managed to get from his place to Chloe's house so quickly as he didn't have a car.

'Maybe he took a taxi.' My answer didn't seem to satisfy him and they kept questioning me. They didn't know and nor did I that Nick had driven Antony to the house.

Now my mind went wild. I saw all kinds of scenarios. A demented man, a stranger, was rushing in from the street, through the front door, brandishing a knife.

'It is possible. Of course,' I said. All things are possible. 'Yes, I suppose a madman might have walked in off the street, but I just don't believe that happened. I really think Antony did it.'

Hiding

The next two days were a blur. My friend Rachel Griffiths arrived from Los Angeles. On the phone, I told her not to make the trip. She had recently nearly died herself giving birth to her third child; she'd had to have three blood transfusions. She was pale. 'You would do it for me,' she said when she walked in the door. Then she said, 'Nick was killed by entitlement.' She had met his children only once, at the Waterlows' beach house.

My friend Marta Garciá-Carrió arrived. 'This day had to come,' she said. 'I told Nick so many times he had to do something but he wouldn't listen.' She reminded me that years ago she, Nick and I and another friend, Father Steve Sinn, had been to see a two-person South African play in a pub in Woolloomooloo. Antony played the role of a son who killed his father. After the play, the four of us had a drink in the pub. Marta was horrified and she kept asking Nick how he felt about seeing his son playing

11

...ch a role. 'It's fine,' Nick had said. I remember Antony being very wooden and rigid on stage. I just thought he wasn't a natural actor.

Steve accompanied me to the apartment because I wanted to find a photograph of Nick for the funeral card. There was a press photographer waiting in the street outside the apartment. As we entered the building the photographer came to the door and said, 'Can I ask a few questions?'

'There's no point,' said Steve, closing the door.

Nick's black Volley sneakers were leaning on the banister in the hallway where he had left them after our last walk— the grass was still on their soles. I opened the blue door and in the hallway on a sideboard stood a large glass vase filled with dead sunflowers. Steve did something that was unforgettable. Composed, and in silence, he took the dead sunflowers out of the vase. He didn't ask me to tell him where the bin was. He just did it. He went down to the street and found the green bin. Then he washed the vase in the kitchen sink. An act of defiance? It was a gesture of hope that made contact with my soul—and whispered, 'Death has no power over us.'

I went through the drawers and shelves, muttering and praying, 'Where are the photos? Please help me find one.' I no longer remembered where anything was kept and I had forgotten how to look for anything. At last I found some discs, and Steve and I sat in front of the computer and we went through them. They were of our travels to Venice, the forest on the south coast of New South Wales; there was a silly one of Nick at the beach wearing a necklace of seaweed, and one of him wearing a snorkel and a mask in front of a gum tree.

'You did lots of nice things together,' Steve said.

'Yes.'

One photo of Nick in Istanbul reminded me of my friend Tina's observation. When Nick was visiting her there she noticed he was always rocking on his heels and she said, 'It was as if he was trying not to fall down.'

'It was hard to take a good picture of Nick. There are not many photos of us together,' I said.

'That's a good sign,' said Steve.

I found some of Nick in front of the Monets at the Musée de l'Orangerie in Paris.

'What about that?'

'Out of focus,' said Steve.

As I scrolled through the images in iPhoto I saw things in Nick's face I hadn't noticed before. I noticed the anxiety in the rut between his brows, and also I sensed something deep within him, something frozen. When we first met I had given him a story I had written about a friend of mine, Roland Topor. I had written how touched I had been when I saw that Roland was as white as a sheet when he got out of a car after a trip to Stockholm. Nick told me that story made him think I would be able to understand his own very vulnerable self. Looking at those photos I thought I didn't realise quite how vulnerable Nick actually was. In those photographs I saw a more fragile soul, and a kind of emptiness within. As I flicked through the years, I saw a man looking more and more exhausted.

The photos in front of the Monets were all out of focus except one: it was of Nick gazing obliquely out of frame, wearing his black baseball cap and brown moleskin jacket, standing in front of the pale pink and green waterlilies.

I quickly grabbed a few things I thought might be useful to help me with the funeral: Nick's jazz CDs, some Thelonious Monk and Coltrane's *Love Supreme*, and Nick's A4 notebook which was on our bedside table. I tossed them on the floor by the front door to make sure I wouldn't forget them. Steve picked up the notebook and was looking through it. He pointed to a page of Nick's jottings: there were meetings and thoughts, people's names, revealing a busy life and a most eclectic range of interests and concerns. 'This page is Nick!' He suggested it as an image for the funeral card. Then he found the list in Nick's handwriting entitled *A Curator's Last Will and Testament*.

We were in the apartment for about two hours, and when we left the building I had forgotten about the photographer. I looked across the street and stood stock still, like an animal, hypnotised by the telephoto lens. It seemed to take ages before I saw the man on the other side of the street or registered what he was doing, and then I grabbed Steve's arm and tried to duck behind him.

Steve and Nick had been friends for many years and I knew Nick respected him greatly. Each time Nick returned from Sunday mass he would walk in the door and say, 'I *love* Steve.' Over the years Steve had come to dinners and parties at our apartment and he made us all feel comfortable in his relaxed and easy presence. But I didn't know him very well. I was a little shy, in awe of him. I'd always called him Steve but now he wasn't just a friend, he was helping me as a priest, so I asked him, 'What should I call you, Father Sinn or Steve?'

He looked at me as if to say, 'What do you think?' and without reproach said, 'Steve!'

•

Over the next few days, friends arrived at the Waller house. I hardly knew they were there. Friends later told me they had been to visit but I couldn't remember having seen them. Jane brought me a bunch of lotus flowers and we went for a walk to nearby Nielsen Park. From a tree, she picked a branch with brick-red flowers and held it out over a crack in the bitumen road. 'Look. This is the story,' she said.

We walked into the park, and Jane showed me the place where she had held a funeral service for her son Jasper. At the beach we stopped at a bubbler and Jane suggested that it would make a nice shrine for Nick outside his gallery, a 'Waterlow bubbler'. She turned the tap and the water sprayed sideways into her face. 'But a better design than this.'

The world is a small stage. This was the same park where Nick had run into a friend ten years before, after I had had my first argument with Antony. I had driven to Nick's apartment to visit Antony without telling Nick. I told Antony to treat his father with more respect. Suddenly a monster appeared before my eyes. His eyes turned red like hot coals and he screamed at me with a raw, guttural cry. I had never before encountered anyone with so much fury. Shaking and terrified, I ran away. Antony had called Nick on his mobile to complain about my visit, and Nick told my friend about the incident. My friend had said to him, 'Juliet has no business interfering with your children.'

Now as Jane and I walked along a lonely bush path, I became frightened. Antony still hadn't been found. I imagined him suddenly appearing out of the bush, rushing towards me.

It was low tide, and we picked our way down to the harbour's edge, sat on the double rocks and looked across the sparkling water towards the bridge in the distance.

Jane said, 'Grief comes in waves; the wave knocks you over, but then it goes away and allows you to stand up again before the next wave arrives.'

I don't remember any waves. I just remember being in incredible pain, so much pain that I no longer existed. I could see the world but I felt as if I had left it. Time both sped up and slowed down. I was walking with feet of stone, on the edge of a dream. And from this dream I had to organise a funeral.

•

I met Steve at his office at St Canice's church in Elizabeth Bay. We sat at his desk; there was space enough for two chairs in a room jam-packed with objects—books, icons, a miniature of the Pietà, a Buddha, paintings and weavings, photographs of friends, street people and others, and a crucifix. The entire room was taken up with a large round table on which papers were piled high, weighted with all manner of objects and books and notes. It seemed to me that all life was in that small office; in it, there was room for everything in the world: God, the spirit life and the human. A box of tissues was perched on a pile of books, and I stared at the penguins on the box. I clung to them. How I wanted to be down there in the Antarctic, lying spreadeagle, face down, on the ice with those indescribably strange human-like birds. I heard Steve's voice. 'I don't know how you're going to manage.'

Those were the kindest of words because they didn't try to steal my grief or push it aside or hide it. They acknowledged my pain, and the bare fact that it was me who would have to manage it—there was no way to avoid grief, and no one else could do it for me.

•

Camilla and my friend Kate Kennedy spent a day visiting various funeral parlours. When they told me about it I was so glad I didn't have to do it. I could not have done it.

'Choosing a coffin is like choosing a car,' said Steve gently.

I thought about the last car Nick had bought for himself. He had gone to a lot of trouble to choose it—a Honda Jazz. It was simple and small and black—and it was the car he had driven his son to the site of his death.

In August 2009 the Ivan Dougherty Gallery had presented the work of a number of contemporary designers, among them a New Zealand-based artist, David Trubridge. David had also given a talk at the college and Nick was upset that I had missed it. He thought I would be interested in David's work and philosophy and I remembered him showing me some pictures, one of which was a photograph of David standing beside a prototype of a coffin standing on its end. The coffin was constructed from sections of recycled plywood held together with jute.

I emailed the dean of the college and asked him to find out if we could purchase one. He came back soon after and said it was possible. It would have to be sent from New Zealand and fumigated; they could do it in time but only if we decided quickly.

I rang Steve and asked him to open the website where he could view the range of coffins that included David's.

I opened the site on Fiona's computer. I read their statement: *At State of Grace we understand that death is a natural part of life.*

I heard Steve's laugh through the receiver. 'I love the name of the site.'

'Click on Caskets,' I told him, 'and scroll down.'

I was doing the same. The first was a basket, woven from willow, like a picnic basket only in the shape of a coffin. Another looked like an icy transparent plastic shroud. It was named *Stunning Silk Cocoon.*

'We won't be getting the shroud,' said Steve.

One called *Return to Sender* was made of cardboard; it looked as if it could be purchased and mailed at the post office.

David's coffin was described as a *Ply and Jute Vessel.* It resembled a giant seed pod. Looking at the image on the screen, I wasn't so sure: I couldn't imagine the seed pod being carried by the pallbearers down the steps of St Mary's Cathedral.

'Jewish coffins are very nice,' said Steve. 'They're plain and have rope handles instead of the ornate brass ones, which just end up in the fire.'

I googled *Jewish coffin* and saw an image of a simple unpainted box. Nick would have approved. I asked Camilla to call the funeral home and order the coffin unpainted. The funeral home called her back to tell her that Jewish coffins were normally painted black, and she asked me was I certain that I wanted it unpainted. I said, 'Yes.'

'But it's just chipboard, it's not even wood. It's not pine,' warned Camilla.

I said, 'Don't paint it.'

To be on the safe side I called Steve. He was aware of the Jewish tradition and said, 'It must be painted black.'

In a panic Camilla made a call to the funeral parlour telling them to paint it!

•

I took a stem from the bunch of lotus flowers and when I arrived at St Canice's church I gave it to Steve. He went to find a vase in the flower room; he brought out some tall metal vases and, from inside them, he pulled bottles of sacramental wine. 'These are hidden from Darko,' he said. Steve chose a tube-like vase, put the lotus flower in it and placed it in front of the Statue of the Sacred Heart on the side altar near the columbarium. The white petals glowed in the dark alcove.

It would not be long before Darko's ashes would be placed under Nick's with the inscription in Latin: *May the angels lead you gently into paradise.* I had met Darko when I first went to the church to discuss the funeral. It was mid-morning. A tall noble figure was standing at the open door. His raw face looked as if it had weathered many storms. As I approached he gave me a wide beautiful smile. Darko was Steve's friend and he lived in a room next to his office. Steve introduced us and Darko started to sing, 'Julia, Jul . . . ia, Julia.' He had been drinking.

'He'll be doing that for a while now,' said Steve, shuffling through his papers.

'Have you ever been to Julia's Creek?' said Darko at the door of Steve's office.

'Darko's been all over the country,' said Steve.

Darko was an artist and Steve had asked him to paint the Stations of the Cross in the church. The hot blue skies, the vivid enamel colours of the figures and Darko's naive touch brought to those agonising scenes an urgent pathos.

He used to man the garage for the Sunday midday mass. He'd sit on a chair in a patch of sun, behind an open newspaper, with his long legs stretched out in front of him; as a parishioner's car swung in, he would mark it with a biro on his thumb and cross it off again when it left.

One morning I asked him if he had been doing any painting lately and he looked up at me, his face ridged with pain. 'No.'

'Why not?'

He replied, 'I've lost the will.'

We squeezed hands and agreed to have a schooner or two up at the pub. We never did. That winter he died of double pneumonia.

•

I told Steve I thought it would be nice to have Nick's funeral under a giant tree.

'Nice idea,' he said. 'But it might be windy.'

'What about the Opera House? He loved that building. We often used to go there to look at it at night.'

'Yes, it's a beautiful building but where would we put the coffin? Let's go and take a look at it, and we can call in at the cathedral on the way.'

We entered St Mary's by the side door and sat in one of the front pews. When I looked up at the vaulted ceilings far above, at the carved red cedar arched beams, I thought, 'This is beautiful.' The yellow sandstone seemed to hold the sun. And there, carved into the white marble of the altar, was the body of Jesus lying on his side, his arms crossed over his chest.

'What would you like him to wear?' said Steve.

'Wear?' His leather jacket, his baseball cap? Black tie? I thought of the Ancient Egyptians. 'I don't know.'

'Or he can just be wrapped in a white sheet.'

'Yes, let's just do that.'

I told Steve that I thought Nick had converted to the Catholic faith.

'I didn't know that,' he said.

Nick hadn't left any instructions for his funeral and sitting in that cathedral made me think he should have a Catholic service. 'How does a Catholic have a funeral?' I asked.

'Normally it's a mass, and they call it a funeral mass or a requiem mass.'

'Let's call it a requiem mass.'

I looked back down the nave of the cathedral, and raised my arm with a flourish. 'And I want jacaranda flowers strewn all the way down the aisle.'

Steve made no comment.

That evening I called him to say what a silly idea that was. 'People will walk on them and bruise them, and there will be a mass of mushy petals and then on the way out they'll slip and fall.'

'Yeah, we wouldn't want a hospital ward full of broken legs,' said Steve.

Nick helped me make so many decisions; he corrected my work, chose my poems, crossing out words and telling me when he wasn't convinced. And now I had to make every decision on my own. I wondered how I would manage without his approval or support.

In my car on the way back from the city Bob Dylan was playing. Nick didn't like his voice. Nick and I didn't have everything in common: he liked Dr John's lived-in voice and voodoo chants, but he wasn't fond of the sexual screams of Prince or Frank Zappa's witty tempestuous orchestral scores, which I loved to play at full volume. I can still hear him saying, 'Turn it down.' And the first thing Nick did when I left the apartment to do some shopping was put on Coltrane. I was fortunate to know a truly great sax player, Eddie Bronson.

I called Eddie from my mobile.

'A funeral in a cathedral . . . I should think of the people and play something soft and respectful.'

'No. Eddie. I want you to play to Nick. Find his soul, his spirit and play something wild . . . like Coltrane. He loved Coltrane.' I played him a CD over the phone, not realising it was Coltrane's spiritual call to God. 'Something like this,' I said.

'Ah, "A Love Supreme",' said Eddie. 'All right. I understand. I will play. I remember watching him when I came to your house. I noticed something very special about him. You sound strong, that is good. Don't worry, my saxophone will cry for Nick.'

I remembered a folk saying from *A Little Book of Jewish Wisdom* I had given George for his thirteenth birthday: 'Pray that you will never have to suffer all that you are able to endure.' Until now my life was just a silly game.

The highlight of my week used to be taking George to Eddie's room in Bondi Road for his clarinet lesson after school. While Eddie played the keyboard and George accompanied him on the clarinet, I passed the time reading a dog-eared illustrated children's book of Bible stories. Eddie had so much patience. One afternoon during the lesson George was staring out the window dreaming and Eddie turned to me and said, 'Oy, you should have more children. They would all be angels like him.'

One afternoon we could hear the telephone ringing from the apartment above. Eddie laughed. 'The man upstairs died a month ago and the telephone has been ringing ever since.'

•

On our way to the morgue, I was sitting in the back seat of the church's battered old hatchback, and I leant forward and asked Shona, Nick's niece, why Chloe had thought it safe to invite Antony to her house.

'Chloe thought Antony wouldn't do anything in front of the children,' she said.

I felt the anger rising through my body. 'Oh, there was far too much stereotyping in that family. What nonsense, stereotyping mothers, grandfathers. "A mother is divine—a mother is safe."' I remember Chloe telling me before she had her first child: 'It would be so nice to be a grandfather.' I told her, 'There is no such thing as a grandfather. There are men who happen to be grandfathers, and women who happen to be mothers. And each one is different. Some might like being a grandfather and others might like it some of the time, or not at all.' My back was on fire and so were my feet. I was angry with Nick, too. Why would such an intelligent man ignore all those warnings, all the threats over so many years, and let Antony in his car? Why was he so careless with his life?

•

When I was in the viewing room in the morgue, I noticed a chair in the corner, and I sat down, exhausted. After a while I heard a soft knocking on the door. It opened, and the counsellor came in. She asked me if I thought the corpse looked like Nick.

'Yes.'

I wondered why she had asked me that. Had she or someone else done a lot of work on him? I couldn't tell where his wounds were under his cotton gown. Perhaps she was asking me to identify him. Then she knelt down beside my chair and softly said, 'You can have any funeral you want for him. Remember, you're next of kin.' Then she rose and left the room. She had such a kind face. I felt I had been visited by an angel in a Bellini painting, an angel who had walked through a doorway to give me a message.

I had been in the room a long time and Steve and Shona were out in the waiting room together. Had they been talking about the funeral arrangements? What had prompted the counsellor to come in and give me that message?

•

I learnt that there was a lot of pressure from the family of Nick's first partner to have a double funeral for Nick and Chloe. Different members of the family started to call me to tell me that this was what should happen. I had already told Steve very firmly that I did not want this, because I believed Nick would not have wanted it. To have a double funeral would only emphasise the fact that they died together, and heighten the tragedy, and I knew that would be done well enough, on the day, by the press. I wanted Nick's funeral to celebrate his life, for it to be as simple as we could make it, as Nick would have wished, and for it to focus as much as possible on his love. It was already a tragedy. How to remember Nick was the most important thing, and I wasn't going to undertake this thing lightly. I wanted people to mourn, and to come away with something good, to take away with them Nick's gift—a real and lasting sense of the love Nick had brought to his useful life. He and his daughter had lived very different lives and they were very different people. That was one of the most important things to acknowledge.

While we were organising the funeral, my sister Camilla said, 'Nick can't have been a humble man, having such a large funeral.'

'He's not organising it; I'm not inviting anyone,' I told her. 'I don't have any address book, only the handful of telephone numbers on my mobile.' Nick had contributed selflessly to the community, and I also knew how many people loved him, and that the cathedral would be filled. The mourners would come because they wanted to (and they did—two thousand of them, and most of them were weeping).

I said to Camilla, 'Anyway, if it was to be a double funeral, who would organise it? Who would choose the music, the flowers, or the coffin? Ben? He chose "Here Comes the Sun" by Nina Simone for Chloe. Nick didn't like Nina Simone.'

As it turned out, there could not have been two more different funerals.

A mound of red roses covered Chloe's ornate mahogany coffin. Chloe's bridesmaids, who only three years earlier had been in the same church, in cocktail dresses, were there again, sombrely attired. And they filed up to the microphone, one by one, to share their memories of their dear school friend.

I knew Nick would not have wanted anything at all on his coffin, and certainly not a floral arrangement. At least once a week he would bring home flowers: deliberating for a long time before making his choice and then always asking for a few simple stems with no greenery. He bought jonquils in spring, garden roses in summer, and very early in spring he would come up the stairs cradling in his arms two-foot-long stems of pink apple or white almond blossom.

Nick and I met during his favourite time of year in Sydney: spring, when the jacarandas are in bloom and the streets are filled with blue clouds. When he came for lunch I served him fish cakes and a rice pudding, which I had forgotten about in the oven. Despite its blackened top, Nick was delighted with it, and he had two helpings. He noticed the jacaranda in bloom through the office window, and another in the garden. The view from the kitchen looked back towards Bellevue Hill, which was dotted with splashes of blue. In part, we might have been brought together by those jacarandas. He told me then that he always had to live with a jacaranda nearby. 'One day,' he said, 'I'm going to buy myself a jacaranda-blue pullover.' He never did.

Nick died at his favourite time of year when the jacarandas are in bloom. When we went for our last morning walk I asked him to stop with me under a tree for a few moments, and we looked up and admired a cluster of blue flowers.

When I saw the dean of COFA he said, 'Nick has ruined jacarandas for me forever.'

•

I still needed to organise the venue for the wake. I wanted it to be at an art gallery, and preferably a contemporary gallery. The Art Gallery of New South Wales was the obvious choice because the mourners could walk from the cathedral to the wake. I didn't want them to have to get into their cars, and separate. They needed one another, and they needed to stay together. The director was overseas and the person who was in charge said he could give me eighty percent permission. I was frantic. Only eighty percent? I called gallery owner Roslyn Oxley and said, 'Help me. How do I get the other twenty percent?' She said she would get back to me. The next day she rang and said it was done. I asked her how and she told me that she had made a call to the person in charge, and had simply listened to him as he talked. And he talked for a long time, she said, until at last he talked himself into it. Now we could put the funeral notice in the paper.

Kate offered to help me. She brought some examples of elaborately worded funeral notices. I looked at them with Jane and she said, 'Well, that's good. We know what we don't want.' We wrote a simple notice with very few words. Kate corrected it and added a few words. I cut the words out and sent it back to her. Kate sent me another version, this time longer, and with the advice from the sub-editor of the newspaper that mine was not the correct way to word a funeral notice. I told her I didn't care what the sub-editor thought, and cut it down again and sent it back. She sent it to me once more, adding one word: 'and'. I emailed her. *We are nearly there. If you just cut out the 'and' and put in the comma, we're done.*

The notice read:

Nick Waterlow OAM. All those who knew and loved Nick are warmly invited to celebrate and grieve a remarkable life. At location St Mary's Cathedral, College Street, Sydney, Friday 20 November 2009, 11 am. Please no flowers. Come in the spirit of jacaranda, bring a sprig!

I had been up all night working on it. Kate told me, 'I do not understand you.' I felt everything depended upon the wording of the funeral notice. Nothing was going to deter me from doing it 'Nick's way'. The notice would stand out among the other, long-winded, more sentimental notices, and it had to carry Nick's spirit. I felt as if I was being driven by Nick's spirit, inside of me, and I was no longer the impulsive, impatient Juliet but a methodical Nick, considering every word carefully, paring it back to the essential, and allowing for space, just as Nick did with his shows and his writings. Nick was always looking for what he could leave out.

I knew Kate had gone to so much trouble. But it was no time for giving in. She was right, she didn't understand me. And I was discovering more about myself. Perhaps she thought I was going mad. Maybe I was.

•

Camilla went back to the apartment to go through Nick's papers to find his birth certificate or passport, but she kept finding childhood photos of Antony, and not finding the papers. Feeling miserable, she heard my telephone ring. It was Eddie Bronson. She didn't answer the phone, and Eddie, on his saxophone, played his song for the funeral, 'Body and Soul', on the answering machine. Camilla said, 'It was beautiful. It made me feel a lot better.'

•

The Waller family were peaceful and harmonious. The house itself was run like clockwork, every blade of grass was trimmed on the green rug of a lawn, laundered and ironed shirts were delivered, gardeners and cleaners arrived and went. The sweet-natured little dog was picked up for its walk and dropped off. I felt I was in one of those perfect houses in the sitcoms that are run by many invisible hands. Fiona was placing the most exciting and beautifully prepared food in front of me every evening, after returning from a day in an operating theatre, managing homework and the schedules of a family of four. She did this effortlessly, and with pleasure. Her family sat cheerfully at the dinner table and I was unable to eat anything. Into this house I had brought so much pain. A year later I ran into Fiona's mother in a doctor's waiting room, and I told her how grateful I was to her daughter and family for inviting me into their house, and for allowing their young children to be exposed to all that grief. 'It was good for them,' she said.

•

Nick and I heard someone singing in the park, and he had commented: 'A solo voice, that would be beautiful at a funeral.' Nick had such poetic ideas. I had heard the most beautiful solo voice eight years earlier at a memorial service, and I had never forgotten it. I remembered only that it had been the voice of a Jewish cantor. I set out to see if I could find someone who could sing like that.

I knew Ross attended the synagogue in Woollahra and Kate had worked for Jewish families in Melbourne, so I asked them both to try to find someone. Kate asked around in Melbourne, and Ross in Sydney, and they both came up with Joseph Toltz. He wasn't sure if he would sing in a cathedral but he was happy to meet to discuss it. I saw him deliberating, and suggested that perhaps he could sing outside on the steps as the mourners filed out. We met with Steve at Ross and Margaret's house and sat at a table with a glass of wine. Steve worked on the order of the mass while Joseph sang Psalm 121 and then the Jewish memorial prayer for the dead. That was the one.

Steve showed me some beautiful hymns which he had chosen. I told him that I wanted to speak at the funeral. He looked at me undecidedly and reminded me that Nick always complained about the long rambling messages I left on people's answering machines. I had told Steve that Nick used to say to me, 'Can't keep it short, can you?'

'I know, I do that,' I said. 'But I need to speak.' ('He doubts me,' I thought, suppressing my annoyance.) I saw that Steve was trying to protect me from myself. How could he know how important this was for me? This was a time for instinct. I thought, 'If I don't speak at Nick's funeral I might not want to ever talk again.'

I needed to declare in public what until then I had only been able to do privately. Nick's family and some friends of the family behaved as if our relationship didn't really exist, and in order to protect it, we allowed them to hang on to this illusion. We both thought, optimistically, that the resentment of his family would lessen. Instead, as the years passed, it grew. So much so that I began to stop talking about us. I didn't tell anyone I did not know well, or who had not demonstrated genuine support for Nick, myself, or us both.

We even had the disapproval of the tiny 'lollipop lady' who stood at the school zebra crossing each morning. 'He is too old for you,' she told me one day as she took me across the road. And she made it known by her withering gaze as we crossed the street on the way to the park for our morning walk. Nick laughed. He thought she was brandishing her stop sign as if it were for us alone. So we would go the other way, to the park, to avoid her steely gaze.

Two years before Nick died we saw Peter O'Brien, Luke's uncle, in the park, and Nick wanted to wait behind a tree until he had gone. In order to avoid him, we walked home the long way round, past the tennis courts. From the beginning our relationship had an aura of secrecy about it. When my father told me he was surprised not to know more about our relationship I quoted from Matthew: 'Give not that which is holy unto the dogs, lest they trample it under their feet and turn and tear you to pieces.' And he laughed.

We really did have to keep it a secret, for ourselves, and the stars. The secrecy had its positive side; it kept it fresh, and erotic. Each night our relationship began again, but only after we had entered the safety of our apartment, and had closed the door to the world behind us.

Our relationship was ready to be celebrated in public at Nick's funeral. I promised Steve I would write my speech, show it to him first, and if he approved, I would read it. 'No ad-libbing,' I said.

'Let's not make it a talk-fest,' said Steve. 'I did a funeral at the cathedral not long ago and everyone got up and talked about how many goals this guy kicked at school and how many races he had won.'

I asked Ross and our friend John Wolseley to speak and gave them the brief: there was to be no talk about Nick's achievements. 'Make it about the man.'

Joseph was still deliberating. Finally he said, 'I will sing. I will wear my yarmulke in the cathedral, and I'll take it off when I sing.' He would sing on the condition that he must not be filmed. He made the decision, he said, 'Because of the kind of person Nick was.' We agreed that Joseph would sing just before the coffin was carried out. I told Steve, 'Then I want the organ to play something so softly that we can almost not hear it . . . as the coffin leaves.'

In the street, on the way to our cars, I had another question for Steve. 'Does the coffin have to have a crucifix?'

Steve stopped and leant on the boot of a parked car. He lowered his head and after a few minutes of deep thought, he said, 'No.'

•

I began writing my speech at midnight and worked into the early hours of the morning. I took it to a friend's house, and we lay on her bed, and she helped me to edit it. She also helped me design a card to give people at the funeral. I took the list Steve had found in Nick's notebook. While the designer was working on the layout I flicked through the pages of Nick's notepad and came across this, in his handwriting:

A Curator's Last Will and Testament
1. Passion
2. An eye for discernment
3. An empty vessel
4. An ability to be uncertain
5. Belief in the necessity of art and artists
6. A medium—bringing a passionate and informed understanding of works of art to an audience in ways that will stimulate, inspire, question
7. Making possible the altering of perception.

The designer created a beautiful card using this will in white on black with a photograph of Nick standing in front of his beloved Monet, one of my poems—'Pain has a surface'—and, on the back, Nick's sweet signature: *Nick*, surrounded by a circle of nine kisses. Along the edge of the card, in faint grey lettering, were the words from Tolstoy: 'All, everything that I understand, I understand only because I love.'

A presentiment

Twenty years ago I was in the back seat of a car, holding my baby George, and the car skidded on the wet dirt road and spun around a few times. We had no seatbelts, and as the car spun in circles I held on to George tight but I could feel him, in slow motion, leave my arms. There was nothing I could do but watch as the centrifugal force pulled my baby out of my grasp. This was how I felt during those last years with Nick.

I could feel Antony getting closer. That morning of Nick's death, when I opened my eyes I was so happy to see him next to me. I smiled at him, and he just looked back at me. He was too anxious to smile. The black road was getting smaller. It was coming to an end.

Nick had a presentiment and he acknowledged it. In the park two weeks before he died he told me: 'I don't think I will live to be very old.'

'How do you know? I might die before you. You don't know,' I said, hurrying to keep up with his long-legged stride. 'Well then, you must make sure you do whatever you want to do. Do it—while you're alive.'

•

At night, Nick used to undress in our office, in the dark. Sometimes, after waiting for him to come to bed and wondering where he was, I would wander out and look for him. I would find him standing half dressed in the shadows of the room or in the bathroom with the light turned off.

'What are you doing here?'

'I'm thinking. I like the dark. I feel safe in the dark,' he said.

There came a time when Nick didn't feel safe in the dark. I would burst out of a doorway, and he would jump. I used to love our marvellous conversations in the middle of the night. One night I leant over him to see if he was awake, so I could talk to him or love him—I was hovering an inch or two over his face to see if his eyes were open. His eyes weren't open but he must have sensed me because he opened them and he jolted with fright.

'I'm so sorry,' I said. 'I didn't mean to scare you. I was just trying to see if you were awake.'

•

Two weeks before his death, Nick and I went through his storage unit, tossing out mouldy books that had been stored for thirty years to make room for the contents of his office. Nick had been working on a new museum and teaching spaces for the COFA campus—his ten-year labour of love. The government was sponsoring the work, and demolition was about to begin. We were getting ready for his six-month sabbatical. We were going to Paris.

When I went to collect the key to Nick's storage unit, the receptionist told me that Antony had been there that morning. He had a storage unit there too. She told me that Antony had lost his keys again and they had given him a new set. He had lost three sets. She asked me if I could pay for them. I did.

'He was very agitated,' she said.

'Really?' I pointed to my head. 'He has something wrong with him.'

'Oh, I didn't know. What a shame. He's so good-looking.'

'What's that got to do with anything?' I said.

She said, 'Yes, I know, it doesn't, but . . .'

'Fingers crossed nothing happens,' I told her. My fear had been reduced to a child's magical gesture. That's what we were doing now—crossing our fingers.

I saw her typing something into the computer. Later, I told Nick that I was annoyed he hadn't told her about Antony, and that I had had to tell her. I thought Nick should have told this woman his son was capable of violent rages, when he had arranged for Antony to store his belongings there. The woman was alone in a tiny office in that aerodrome of a storage facility. What if she had insisted that Antony pay for his key? What might have happened then?

On one of our last walks I asked Nick, 'Do you think Antony will ever get better?'

'No,' he said firmly.

From his storage unit, Nick had taken a few keepsakes and brought them home—a large framed black-and-white photograph of Antony as a young boy, and a few small pictures of his father with himself as a baby. He put them all on his desk. On the day of Nick's murder Antony's photo was lying face up on his writing desk. When Steve came back to the apartment after our visit to the morgue, I gave it to him. 'Can you get rid of this?' He nodded and took it away.

Another evening, at an opening, Nick was talking to an art journalist about the building at COFA. On the way out I told Nick that I didn't think he should have talked so openly to the journalist. Earlier in the year I had been interviewed by this man, and I didn't think he was someone to be trusted. Nick took my suggestion very badly, and on the way home he raised his voice, telling me that I didn't know what I was talking about. I was trying to protect him but he accused me of not respecting him. I didn't say a word but as I was slowly turning the car around to park it in the street Nick shouted something I had never heard him say in our ten-year relationship: 'You are irrelevant!'

I took my foot off the accelerator, and let the car gently roll forward until it collided with the base of an old camphor laurel.

'What did you do that for?' he said.

•

The weekend before Nick died we flew to Canberra for the day because he especially wanted to see an exhibition by artist Aida Tomescu. The white space was filled with fiery blood-red paintings—thick oil cadmium red, orange and yellow impasto looked as if it had been slashed tempestuously across the canvases, some with lines incised into the caked surface as if they had been made with claws. I sensed they made Nick uncomfortable. He had long admired the artist's work and so I was surprised when he said he wanted to leave a short time after we arrived. As we walked out he told me he preferred her earlier works—the calmer blue, green and white works, two of which were hanging in the entrance.

We walked to the National Gallery, and Nick sought out two paintings: *Suddenly the Lake* by Rosalie Gascoigne, and *Victory Over Death No. 2* by the great New Zealand artist Colin McCahon. I had asked Nick in 2005 if there was any painting in Australia that he would go to see that would console him and uplift him. He said it would be the painting *Victory Over Death No. 2*, with 'I Am' at the centre of the canvas, because it acknowledges the most extraordinary doubt, but ultimately it authenticates the artist. It's very spare, it's simple, but somehow it talks of ever-lasting truth, and gives one great reassurance in the face of everything that may come one's way.

At one in the afternoon we went out into the sculpture garden, to the fog sculpture by Japanese artist Fujiko Nakaya. We sat on a bench talking while a gentle breeze lifted the vaporous waters and sent them drifting sideways through the grove of casuarinas; their dark forms gradually disappeared from view, and moments later, when the wind changed direction, they would suddenly appear again. 'I have to see Antony,' Nick said.

I went for a walk around the sculptures in the garden and when I returned I looked at Nick slumped on the bench.

'You look so tired,' I said. 'We have to spend more time in nature.' We sat in silence among the moving shadows, under the casuarinas, listening to the warbling of the magpies.

Our last dance

I am wearing the wedding ring Nick has never seen. He had asked me to marry him in Amsterdam by the canal. 'Ask me again later,' I said.

'I can only ask and get rejected so many times,' he said.

'I'll marry you,' I said. 'But I want things to clear up with your kids first.' I didn't want to add fuel to the envy I felt from his children and I didn't want to aggravate Antony.

I could only play three songs on the piano. One of them was the beautiful Thelonious Monk melody 'Ask Me Now'. As I played the interior rhythms I hoped and wondered when the time would come when I would feel ready to say that to Nick. The time had come. I ordered the ring two weeks before.

On his last morning Nick was in front of the bathroom mirror. I came up behind him.

'Do you like this secret relationship?' I said. 'Is it good for you?'

He didn't answer.

'It makes it more erotic. But I feel ready to make it more public. I know that nothing is going to change and I don't care. I want to marry you. Still, we are going to have to marry in secret . . . in Paris.'

Nick didn't say anything.

'Do you still want to marry me?'

I could see his face in the mirror. He nodded. He was solemn. He was often that way. I had told him so many times that I felt we were already married, and he had said he felt the same way. In his speech at Chloe and Ben's wedding reception he'd mentioned that Chloe and Ben had had a child out of wedlock, and he said that for him, marriage wasn't important—the important thing was the commitment.

Nick never told me about the email that had been sent to him in 2007 by Gaye Bell, Antony's friend and landlord, detailing Antony's history of physical and verbal violence from May 2004 until 13 May 2007; a list that had also been sent to the doctors at St Vincent's Hospital. He didn't mention the letter dated January 2007 from Gaye to the doctors describing Antony's bizarre paranoid and violent behaviour, questioning why the doctors continued to believe that therapy was the appropriate means of convincing Antony to take his medication. She wrote to the doctors that she did not believe Antony would ever take his medication. And Nick didn't tell me that he had contacted the hospital to alert them to the fact that Antony had threatened him with a knife.

That last morning Nick didn't tell me he was seeing Antony that afternoon.

•

And I didn't tell him about the ring.

I asked Camilla and Fiona to collect it for me from the master jeweller Robb Gardner so I could wear it to the funeral. Camilla told me that when Robb opened the box to show them the ring Fiona burst into tears. The box came with a card from Robb with the words: *I am so very sorry*.

•

The Saturday evening before the Monday night Nick died, we were at the Bacchus Ball at the University of New South Wales campus. The dean and his wife held out their hands to show us their matching wedding rings. 'They cost a lot,' said the dean with playful irony. Richard Neville, the emcee, brought a bottle of champagne to our table, and Nick popped the cork exuberantly.

Nick looked very distinguished in his Savile Row black tie and I wore a long black dress. Overweight elderly academics were wandering about in the dimly lit room wearing Greek togas and olive wreaths in their hair. The music was good. We danced as we always did, abandoning ourselves and one another to the music; Nick with his own very special way of dancing, his knees slightly bent, kicking the air and rocking his pelvis 'in ways that suggested a psychedelic go-go dancer', as one of the obituaries put it—to his own imagined syncopated rhythms. As we were dancing, I called out above the up-tempo numbers, 'I love the way you love life—life itself.' We danced that night as if it was our last dance. We had always danced that way—and that was the way we had always loved.

A man seated on my left, who worked in administration at the art school, told me he was lucky to be there as his father had just died. He told me he'd thought he wouldn't be able to go to a ball with death on his mind. I told him, 'I think about death every single day.' He asked me if Nick had any plans to retire.

'Nick will never retire,' I said. 'He wants to work forever.'

I leant over to Nick and whispered in his ear, 'That man on my left is wondering when you're going to retire. I told him, "Never."'

'That was a good reply,' said Nick.

Nick's pocket diaries

Meticulously and in tiny handwriting, Nick entered into his annual *Economist* Pocket Diary what he ate, what lectures, meetings and openings he attended, his cholesterol levels, telephone numbers, who he met, and what delighted and inspired him.

Walked in Centennial Park, watched Roman Holiday, *osso bucco.*

Beautiful flathead again!

In bed with JD!

Beautiful day.

Another beautiful morning! T-bone and red wine. Starry starry night!

On the inside cover he wrote quotes. In his 2009 diary was a line of dialogue from my unpublished story 'Mercy Annie': *Remember no one else knows what it is you need.*

A quote by Thomas à Kempis from *The Imitation of Christ: If you have seen any man die think that you yourself shall go the same way. Wherefore be ever ready and LIVE so that death find you never unready.*

Art is always a question. Propaganda is an answer.

One from Alexander Solzhenitsyn: *Falsehood can hold out against much in this world but not against art.*

I had to be artistically free, not confronted by a God hard as steel like the Assyrian kings, but with the God inside of me, glowing and holy like the love of Christ: Emil Nolde, 1914. *To live is to change, and to be perfect is to have changed often:* Cardinal Newman. A silly one that Nick might have seen in the street: *Please do not throw stones at this notice.* The words from Jeff Nuttall, which I heard him repeat so often: *The certainty of uncertainty twisting in your guts.* And the most beautiful one from Van Gogh: *The more I think it over the more I feel that there is nothing more truly artistic than to love people.*

Did Nick know he was going to die? Was he ready to die—on his feet?

Many years ago I had been given some river stones by a dear friend, and I had brought them back from New York and for years I kept them in a bowl in the hall. One day I decided to clean up and Nick saw me throwing them out. 'But this man loved you, and you're going to just throw them out?' he said disapprovingly.

'They're just stones,' I said.

'You don't care?' He was concerned.

Nick inscribed his name and his love for me inside the covers of all the books he gave me. One day I said, 'Do you have to write in all the books? I might want to give them away.' He looked hurt. How I wish I hadn't said that.

For ten years he had left scattered about our apartment little love notes and cards.

Dearest Juliet, Above all, I love you, every little bit of you, in every way. As always, he signed it *Nick*, and surrounded his name with a ring of kisses.

I love your cooking.

I love you very much. 6.45 pm.

Dearest Juliet, I love the beauty of you and your soul, with my love always, Nick.

Dearest Juliet, I love your freedom, spontaneity and abandon. Nick.

Oh, I love you in the midst of all this, in the midst of everything.

And after his death I found this by the bed:

You are so beautiful within and without, original, iconoclastic, loving, singular and unique, funny, outrageous, tender, passionate, deeply discerning, poetic, gritty, ballsy, brave, tender, vulnerable, beguilingly honest, wilful, spontaneous, combustible, irresistible, multi-talented, an acute observer and recorder of people and events others overlook, modern yet loving of tradition that endures, delicate, open and full of wonder, from the intensity of suffering and pain your spirit is indomitable and soars above the humdrum and mediocre, you are the most precious of flowers.

Many times every day he also told me how much he loved me. Often he had tears in his eyes when he said it. I loved hearing those words although I didn't need to be told. I knew it.

We fell in love—fell is not quite the right word; expanded is better—at a cafe in a bookshop near his work. In that one holy hour it seemed we talked about everything. Immediately discovering so many things about each other. We were both outsiders. We felt we had already talked about everything, said everything there was to say; it was as if we had already been a part of one another's lives. Our conversations were more like recollections.

He looked at me seriously. 'I need one person, just one person to love and be loved by.'

And, as our mutual friend the English-born artist John Wolseley (once an inmate with Nick at a preparatory school in the far reaches of East Anglia) had predicted before he introduced us, our humour did come together—and collide. The world was already ridiculous, as was our place on this earth; on top of that we saw absurdity in every living thing: in a mad flickering leaf, a person's funny walk, in the way someone impatiently ripped off his scarf while giving a lecture on a stage. We laughed at such ordinary things that we needed nothing special to entertain us. Sometimes in the middle of the night we would find ourselves laughing so loudly and uncontrollably that in the hallway the following morning our neighbour would ask what it was that we had found so funny. We had so many things in common and I thought Nick was a person who would share everything with me.

'But he didn't tell me he was seeing his son that evening,' I cried to the homicide detective on the telephone.

'We can't tell each other everything,' he said kindly. 'We all have to protect ourselves.'

•

The last year of Nick's life was like a slow-moving dream. Events were taking place but just behind time. Nick had stopped talking to me altogether about his children, and I didn't talk to others about our life together: we were enveloped in a kind of silent fog.

Nick began to leave me cards on the kitchen table before going to work. Was he doing this because he knew he was leaving me? He was becoming more and more distracted, and one night he became very upset when he arrived home and found I had left the front door of the apartment unlocked while I was in the bath.

I was beginning to feel worn down by a thing that I couldn't then name—a sense of foreboding. I could feel Nick's heavy burden and a heavier sense of hopelessness. His body was more stooped and bent over. It was like those muggy days when the air is still and hangs heavily and it wants to rain but it doesn't and everything seems to be waiting. Something was going to happen but when and where and how I did not know. I remember telling Nick and others that when Antony's money ran out—and it was clear that it would—'That day will be a bad day.'

The morgue

I was in Fiona's sunny garden when my mobile rang. The phone was hot as it had been in constant use. It was someone from the morgue calling to ask me if I intended to view Nick's body.

'I don't know. Do you think I should?'

'We think it can be a very helpful thing to do, to see him,' said a woman's voice.

Fiona, who is a doctor, told me: 'It is a good thing to do. I'm warning you, he will be cold.'

Steve called to say he would take me to the morgue. It was a very hot day and I arrived at St Canice's wearing a sleeveless day dress, lime-green and printed with a multitude of tiny apples.

Steve's grandniece arrived wanting him to play basketball with her. Steve told her he was sorry but that he couldn't right then. She was disappointed. 'But I have something for you,' he said. He went into the kitchen and I watched him pull a box of doughnuts from the fridge and offer her one. I felt I was peering through a glass window, watching real life in a dream—watching life go on and I was not with them. Steve's grandniece took a doughnut and gave him a kiss. Steve smiled and turned to me. 'Aren't I lucky?' he said.

In the bland foyer of the morgue we were greeted politely by a counsellor and a very tall homicide detective with a young face. I followed them with trepidation into the sky-blue waiting room. I remained poised while the counsellor stood in front of us and explained that Nick was lying on a table in the viewing room. She said that I could touch him if I wanted but that his body would be cold. Her words registered for the first time and I broke. I put my head into my lap and started sobbing. Steve immediately rose and motioned to me to follow him. As he opened the door to the windowless viewing room I was summoned by the sight of Nick's long body lying on a trolley, and at once I stopped crying. I heard the door close softly behind me.

Nick was dressed in a blue cotton gown. He looked as he did in our bed beside me; he always slept on his back. I could see every vein and tense muscle in his face. His hands weren't folded as I had expected them to be; they were by his side.

My eyes searched his body, trying to find his suffering, but there was no sign of it. I put my hand on his chest. It was cold. I touched his grey face very gently, and then I placed my fingers over the long fingers of his right hand, my warm hand on his cold hand. The hand of death.

In bewilderment, I stared for a long time at his inert body. I wanted to run my hands up and down, from his head to his feet, to touch all of him. I wanted to climb up on the trolley, and lie beside him, and take him in my arms and hold him and feel the weight of his body. I might even have contemplated it if I hadn't noticed the security camera in the ceiling and remembered the detective. Perhaps he was watching. It was murder—did they think I was a suspect? Later I said to the counsellor, 'Do you think I could have picked him up and held him? Someone told me dead bodies are very light.'

'No. He would have been too heavy,' she said.

After the funeral, George told me how heavy Nick's coffin was and Luke said he had struggled with it too, even though there were six pallbearers.

I touched Nick's face gently. His eyes had been closed and I wanted to open them. I wanted to see those laughing eyes again.

But he was not there. I told Steve: 'He was not there.'

'I think I understand what you mean. It's a funny way of putting it,' he said.

'That's the whole point of viewing the corpse,' Jane had said. 'You understand they are no longer there.'

In that viewing room I was struck by a deep and profound silence; a silence with a strange full resonance that I knew would never again leave this world.

•

I went back out into the waiting room and sat down next to the homicide detective. He talked to me. I heard him saying, 'Death is difficult.' I looked at his empathetic face—I was astonished that a homicide detective had the courage to say such banal words. He was trying to help me and what he was doing takes an uncommon humility.

After the funeral, my youngest niece Sequoia walked with me up to the local police station where I was to meet with the detective to make my statement for the prosecution.

'Do you find him intimidating?' she asked.

'No. He is one of the most courteous and humble and gracious men I have met.'

'You should tell him that,' she said.

She sat in a nearby park and read a book and waited for me. The detective typed out my statement in the back room of the police station. After an hour I looked at my watch and asked him how much longer it would take because I wanted to drive my niece to the airport. He offered to finish it later. 'If there is one thing to learn from this sad story, it is that we need to look after our children,' he said.

I asked him why he had become a detective. He told me he had switched careers from marketing quite late in life, in his forties, and that it had been a hard decision to make because he had had a good job and a young family to support. But he had always wanted to do it. Being a detective was a career that one could continue to pursue as one got older—'when I can't jump over fences'. And he added, 'It is an honour to work with death.'

•

After we had been to the morgue the detective, Steve and I went back to my apartment. As the detective walked in the door he smiled and said, 'Would you like a cup of tea?'

'Yes. Would you like one?' I smiled back at him.

I put the kettle on. The telephone rang. I answered it and walked into our bedroom. It was our friend John Wolseley, who had introduced Nick and me ten years earlier in that very kitchen.

John's voice sounded different. It was a voice I'd not heard before, it was one for grief: a little higher, more formal and hundreds of years older. I could picture him on his estate in Somerset wearing breeches and a smock. 'Sweet. I'm so sorry.'

It made me weep. 'Oh, John.' I couldn't talk. Nick's teddy with the little heart on its red knitted jumper was on the pillow: it seemed so much smaller than before. His other teddies, one with a broken arm, were on his bureau beside his OAM badge in a glass case. When Nick first moved in my young son was surprised and delighted that Nick, a grown man, a very old man to him, still treasured his teddies.

I offered Steve and the detective a glass of water. I took out the ice bucket and reached for a handful of ice, then stopped myself. As I walked to the sink and picked up the soap I could feel the detective's eyes on me. I held my hands under the running water and thought, 'I have just touched a dead man's body, my lover's body, and I am standing at the very sink where each night, so happily, I used to rinse the vegetables for our evening meal, and now I am about to serve a priest and a senior homicide detective a glass of water on this hot spring day.' I truly knew the meaning of Edgar Allan Poe's poem 'A Dream Within a Dream':

> *Take this kiss upon the brow!*
> *And, in parting from you now,*
> *Thus much let me avow—*

You are not wrong, who deem
That my days have been a dream;
Yet if hope has flown away
In a night, or in a day,
In a vision, or in none,
Is it therefore the less gone?
All that we see or seem
Is but a dream within a dream.

I stand amid the roar
Of a surf-tormented shore,
And I hold within my hand
Grains of the golden sand—
How few! yet how they creep
Through my fingers to the deep,
While I weep—while I weep!
O God! can I not grasp
Them with a tighter clasp?
O God! can I not save
One from the pitiless wave?
Is all that we see or seem
But a dream within a dream?

The funeral

I handed Nick's John Coltrane CD to the driver and asked him to play it on our way to the cathedral. On our laps were large sprigs of jacaranda that Fiona had thoughtfully picked for us that morning. George wore his brown graduation suit, a borrowed shirt and tie, and Nick's brown shoes. He and Nick wore the same size. I had debated between the grey silk Chinese-style dress with soft pink flowers embroidered up one side, which Nick had bought me at Madam Mao's in Shanghai, or a plain black nylon dress with a round neck. I chose the black one. I asked George: 'I wonder if Stas will be there?' In the car I kept an eye out for the jacarandas which would appear every now and then as we turned a corner—blue shadows under blue trees. I might have imagined them. Spring had come earlier this year, and I was worried that there would be no sprigs for people to pick.

The car pulled up outside the cathedral and Stas and his mother were standing just where we stopped. Stas had been George's best friend at primary school; back then he, George, Nick and I had spent so much time together, afternoons, weekends and holidays, but I hadn't seen him since. Stas was a young man now, and tall, but with the same beautiful open moon-shaped face.

Patsy from the funeral parlour was there to greet us and we followed her up the steps and into the cathedral. Felicity from COFA was at the door handing out the funeral cards. We walked down the nave to the altar. Huge branches of jacaranda stood in two giant urns on either side; they looked like a blue forest. Steve came up to me. 'There's the coffin.' I hadn't noticed it.

I walked over to it and around it; I looked at it vacantly and thought, 'What's a coffin doing here?'

There was nothing on it but a small white card, like one from a filing cabinet, with two words: *Nick Waterlow*. The coffin was beautiful, black and archetypal, but I couldn't grasp its significance.

I knew that the cathedral was filling but I couldn't see the congregation. My vision had shortened.

Steve was perspiring under his purple vestments, the colour of which gave new meaning to the flowers in the urns, the sprigs in our hands, and the trees blooming throughout the city. Death was in each particle of every blossom.

Steve's gentle voice, when he gave his homily, filled the air with an intensity that came from great suffering:

We are celebrating this morning a requiem mass for Nick. We don't want to be here, we want Nick to be with us still. We were not ready for his death. We weren't prepared for such an awful, senseless death. But here we are, together, and Nick and Chloe are no longer with us, and Antony has disappeared. It is our human dignity to pray: *Requiem aeternam dona eis, Domine.* Give him eternal rest, Lord.

Mass is a memorial of another death and a celebration of His resurrection. It is the sacrament of His abiding presence in our lives. Many may not be familiar with the responses, or believers in Him. You are not outsiders here, there is no imperialism of faith here. We sit together, human being with human being. With music, words and actions, let us remember Nick and the love that holds us together.

'I was a child of the Sixties,' Nick wrote in his diary, 'the first generation not to be conscripted, and the first generation not to go to war.' Nick spent the last twenty years of his life fighting a different kind of enemy. An elusive enemy that menaced him and his family. It was hidden and it had captured Antony. It was frightening and violent. Nick tried every avenue for peace. He prayed, he sought advice; he never gave up on Antony being freed. He hoped that his love and acceptance would deliver his son from the powerful forces that at times controlled him. He has been defeated. He underestimated his enemy. He lies now, like this marble body beneath the altar, silent and cold, lifeless. What was alive, passionate, inquiring, affectionate, joyous, loving, has been struck down. His worst fears, his deepest anxieties, realised. The sun has darkened, the moon has lost its light, the stars have fallen from heaven and the powers in heaven have been shaken.

We do not shield our eyes from what has happened. We do not close them, or retreat into a world that airbrushes the nightmare. We saw at times his ashen face, his fears and anxieties, his pain and anguish. Our hearts are on hold, our voices silent, our ears closed, our feelings numb, our limbs have given way.

Juliet felt Nick's love in her body. Do you feel his love? There is no defeat in death. His love, like that Love we remember here on this altar, pressed on to the end, and now beyond death.

The lame shall leap like a deer, the tongues of the dumb shall sing for joy. They will come to Sion shouting with joy, everlasting joy on their faces; joy and gladness shall go with them, sorrow and sighing shall flee away.

•

Steve had told us all, he had told the world, something that until then had never been said—Antony's mental illness had been known about for twenty years. To me it had only been acknowledged in the last five years.

•

George was sitting next to me, grounded and still. I felt his good strong energy. Steve motioned for me to rise. I walked up to the pulpit very slowly; my feet were like lead. As I took off my glasses at the lectern so I could read my homily, I suddenly felt so tired I wanted to lie down right there. But Steve's homily had given me eagle's wings, inside of me, to help me stand. I welcomed the congregation, acknowledged Nick's mother and Luke and Ben. And then I thanked George for embracing Nick into his life.

George, Nick and I had recently celebrated George's twenty-first birthday, and I wrote him a poem as a present. When I gave it to George he looked at it and said, 'It's long.' I printed it on blue paper. Before I gave it to George I gave it to Nick; as he was reading it, I saw the tears begin to pour down his face.

After the funeral many people said to me they were surprised that Nick was a religious man. In my homily I had said: 'Nick was a man who could say, "I don't know."' This was one of the many things that made him religious. Point four in his *Curator's Last Will and Testament* was 'The ability to be uncertain'. Faith is not based on certitude. The way Nick lived was open to hope, to faith, without presumption. Artists and priests have this in common, the faith to endure not knowing—they can live in a kind of darkness.

Jane read the poem she had helped me to choose, 'Asking the questions that have no answers'. Nick was always encouraging me to write and he wanted me to publish a book of poems—he had selected them for the book two weeks before his death—so it was appropriate that the first public reading of one of my poems would be at his funeral. Nick and I both delighted in the paradoxes, in those things that tripped our sense of certainty. The sense of 'not knowing' was the reason looking at art with Nick was such a thrill, and it turned everything into an adventure; this was why, as I said in my homily, 'even shopping for milk with Nick was exciting'. If we thought something was going to happen one way, and then the opposite happened, we believed it to be one of the delights of life. But now that Nick is in his coffin I will never again, for a second, think that I 'know' anything. The earth and the heavens will shake and tremble forever with unknowing.

I told the mourners, 'We were two heads and two hearts together.' The first card I gave Nick bore the image of two elephants in profile, their heads pressed together, their two sad eyes level with one another. He had kept this card in his top drawer.

I walked through my speech, one leaden step at a time, hearing my voice echo through the vast cathedral as if it was coming from the other end of the nave. I realised I had come to the last line when I heard myself say: 'Thelonious Sphere' (I had to include his beautiful middle name) 'Monk wrote, "It's always dark or we wouldn't need light."' I straightened up and looked into the darkness of the world and said, 'Nick was my light.'

Numb with shock, I tried not to stumble as I felt my way down the steps. As I passed the coffin bearing Nick's body, silenced forever, I felt the light of incomprehensible love. My whole body was warm with it. I liked those lines from Nick's favourite pianist. Why be afraid of the dark, when it is always dark? In this darkness there is only one light—that is all we have.

John, dressed in a knee-length black coat from an earlier time, spoke with his gentle humour but also with indignation and rage and suffering. He unfolded his speech in a long scroll and it fell to the ground. Ross concluded his eulogy with a poem by Roger Lipsey, and told the congregation that he had added just one word, and left it for us to guess which one. I remembered Nick telling me: 'Ross is nothing if not equivocal.'

Steve celebrated the Eucharist and performed the rituals over the coffin with water and incense with perfect timing: rituals to remind us that death has happened many times before, many times over. In awe, I watched Steve sing the hymns, fervently—with passion. I asked him afterwards, 'How was it that you could sing?'

He said, 'Well, in a way it's my job. When I say it's my job, you get called, as artists are called. I'm amazed they can do it, and put out stuff that has often taken everything they have to offer. But I believe that the community needs certain people: there are doctors, there are teachers—and it needs priests. And you do it on behalf of the community. My job is to, as it were, be a bridge: to present people to God, and offer their prayers to God. And I had that job to do, on that day, to honour Nick, and to do what we human beings do when someone dies. We gather, we remember, we hear the word of God, which is a word of life . . . and we sing. We sing songs of lamentation, of praise, or supplication. We call God down. "Oh come down, our love divine, breathe on me." We want the depth of his presence, we want it, not to come empowered, not to come . . . God almighty—but just breathe on us. Breathe your spirit into our hearts—that's what we sang. So, it's not a God who's in command, or in control, or sitting on a throne, but breathing his spirit on us, and abiding with us. "As the darkness falls, deepens, abiding with us who are helpless and reminding us of his death on the cross."'

Steve said, 'I think it's our great dignity, as human beings, to sing. The Jewish people, on the way to the gas chambers—they would sing. That's claiming our dignity.

Proclaiming that not even death itself has any power over us. I want to think that we can claim our souls in the midst of whatever degradation, whatever violence, whatever cruelty, whatever evil is thrown at us. It is the place to sing, really, isn't it? Death. It's a victory. Saying, "Where, O death, is your victory?"'

•

At one point during the funeral Steve crossed the floor of the cathedral, came up to me, and kissed me on the forehead. I told my sister afterwards that I felt, then, I had been kissed by God. She replied, 'Oh yeah?'

•

There was a longer than usual silent spell, and I was watching Steve who was waiting, with intense focus, in front of the altar, when I suddenly remembered Eddie. It was time for Eddie to play. He was in the pew behind me, waiting for his cue. I stood, and motioned to him with my head. He jumped up, picked up his old saxophone, which he had unpacked and left leaning against the sandstone column, and then he walked slowly over to the coffin. He stepped forward and played to Nick's body enshrouded in its white sheet. And he played to Nick's soul. He began slowly and sweetly, and then he went low, downwards, into the depths, into the darkness—holding the grief and the pain which was bursting inside our veins—and he rose higher and higher, and finally his saxophone screamed: it wailed, it lamented, it pierced the air, and carried with it Nick's spirit up and up to the light, to the heavens, nearly choking with the last of his faltering breath.

An Aboriginal woman walked up the aisle and up to the throne where Steve was sitting poised, motionless. She spoke to him. I saw him nod, and then she went to the microphone. She told us how she had just arrived in Sydney from Dubbo, and that she had never met Nick but he sounded as if he was a great man, and she wanted us to know that she and her people felt connected to him. Then she went on and talked about a train ride and how you had to get off at different stations. Then I lost her. I didn't understand what she was saying.

I thought, 'Nick would have loved the fact that an Aboriginal woman, a stranger, had come into the cathedral and had sabotaged the proceedings at his funeral.' That was a sign to us—there is a spirit.

Joseph Toltz sang the memorial prayer for the dead. I didn't know the Hebrew words. Later, when I read them in English, I was delighted to discover that the prayer for the dead was a hymn of praise to God. Nothing could have been a more beautiful end to the requiem mass.

As if she was absent-mindedly attending to housework, Patsy picked up a stray jacaranda petal from the carpet but then she realised where she was and thoughtfully placed it on the coffin. This prompted me to try to shake the petals from my sprig over the coffin but they didn't fall off, so I placed the whole branch on the coffin. The organ began, just as I had wanted it to, and we could hear the faintest strains of Caccini's 'Ave Maria'. The pallbearers took their places around the coffin, and Patsy showed them how to hold on to one another. With difficulty, all being different heights, they heaved the coffin onto their shoulders. Camilla grabbed my arm, and we followed the procession down the aisle, past a sea of dark blurred faces, which went on, and on, and on.

•

Out in the blinding midday light, Steve, Luke and I blessed the coffin with incense and then we watched the attendants slide it into the back of the hearse. It rolled away down the street with Patsy, in her blue suit and hat, walking in front of it.

The senior homicide detective suddenly appeared out of the crowd to tell me that he and other plainclothes detectives were about. 'I just want to tell you there is nothing for you to worry about,' he said.

The wake

The pathway between St Mary's Cathedral and the Art Gallery of New South Wales was strewn with jacaranda petals. Students from COFA were handing out sprigs to the passing mourners. On the steps of the art gallery, two Aboriginal men were playing the didgeridoo to welcome the mourners. We were banked up at the front entrance and I found myself standing next to Nick's friend Wart, who suffers from schizophrenia. Her telephone number was written on the top of the inside cover of his pocket diary.

I first met Wart at Frank Watters' gallery. We were looking at the paintings when we heard a truck horn blasting from the street. Wart looked out the window and said, 'Some bloody idiot has left their car parked in the middle of the street with the bloody lights on.' Thirty seconds later she said, 'That's my car.' She ran out, got into it and drove off. I saw her again when she crashed George's twenty-first birthday dinner. Nick was delighted to see her and invited her to join us; he fiercely defended her behaviour to George's stepmother, who complained that Wart was an attention-seeker. Wart gave George a branch that looked like a pair of antlers, and George, in celebration of her generous, erratic spirit, put it on his head for her while she took a photograph.

In the crowd Wart looked at me and said, 'Oh, girl, you must be feeling like shit! Antony is mentally ill, but he's a murderer. Us mentally ill people don't kill. Did I tell you when I was in hospital Nick sent me a dozen red roses? I gave one to everyone in the ward.'

Wart sent me this beautiful letter after the blessing:

Hi and Howdee Juliette,
The last time we spoke was at yours and Nick's place and their was such warmth and friendliness tho when I was leaving I hoped you had someone to stay there with you to talk. When Nick died I started writing this piece called 'Unfinished Conversations' and thought that night how lonely you looked. And of course how many of those conversations must be going thru your head.

My brother's wife died a couple of weeks ago and you just realize the fragility of life. The balances, the pulls and sways. Wot was it that Nick would say—Be comfortable in uncertainty.

Your words 'Pain has a surface' is a searing thought—you have amazed me thru the totally extreme nature of violence asserted. And how everyone has reeled in shock, devastation. I look forward to hearing how you are going—and I know—pain hurts. I don't mean to sound flippant. Talk soon. Love Wart.

In the gallery I saw my mother in the crowd and I moved over to her and kissed her on the cheek. She didn't return my kiss. She stood looking at me without speaking. It was the first time I had seen her since Nick died. I looked at her pale face and at that moment I understood that her suffering was greater than I had imagined; hers must have been a terrible, incommunicable pain for surely she must have wanted to offer courage or sympathy to her daughter at such a time. I turned away and faced the crowd.

Nick's niece came up and said that I must come and visit her sometime after she had settled into her new home. She described in detail how difficult it was to be moving house. I was thinking that I didn't care how hard it was for her to unpack boxes in her new home, and that her tribulations were . . . when my spiteful mind was stopped short by Steve's generous words: 'Yes, moving house is very hard.'

Nick's other niece asked me how I felt.

'Like a ghost,' I told her. 'But I can still put lipstick on.'

She laughed. 'Juliet has a wicked sense of humour.'

I wasn't trying to be funny. I was no longer there but at the same time I could see the world as if it was a reflection in a giant mirror. I just couldn't believe it. I couldn't believe anyone, but of course I could.

Hetti Perkins gave me a hug. People I had been success-fully avoiding for years came up and kissed me. A work colleague of Nick's said, 'What a shame!' Within seconds, he was telling me how depressing it was that now he had reached sixty his sex drive was not what it used to be.

Two young women came up and stood in front of me—smiling inanely, like twins from a Diane Arbus photograph.

I looked at them and I couldn't think of anything to say. Another pretty girl looked at me with sympathy in her eyes but her face was completely expressionless. She told me how sorry she was, and I could hear her voice trembling. What was going on here? Then I thought, 'Ah, of course—Botox.'

I could hear Nick's volcanic laughter. Ross had mentioned Nick's laugh in his homily. 'Nick's wonderful laugh. The shock of it. I used to love to induce it.' Ken Unsworth told me that Nick's laugh used to worry him. I asked him to explain this but he wouldn't. 'You must press him,' said Ross. Perhaps he thought it was the nervous laughter of a man who wanted, who needed to laugh. But that would be no different from a man who wanted to love, who loved to love, and sought out what he might love.

People did not know what to say. I did not know what to say. A woman came up to me and told me something about a baby elephant recently born at Taronga Zoo. Someone told me his brother was doing amazing things—importing scented candles. Another told me about the children of a wealthy philanthropist who had given their mother a ghostwriter for her birthday to write her memoir. My uncle talked to me about naming rights for the new COFA gallery. My brother talked to me about money.

I looked over at a nearby art installation by Gregor Schneider: it was a large cage with a blown-up lilo and an open beach umbrella inside it. I wanted someone to put me in there—and lock the gate.

But Nick's death also prompted a searching of hearts. Couples would hold hands in public for the first time in years, and meet with their lawyers to draw up their wills. Young mothers would discipline their children. My mother would resurrect from a dusty cupboard, a photograph of her father taken at twenty-three years of age in uniform, having fought for four years on the western front. Wart would finish her 'Unfinished Conversations', and artist friends would embark on projects they had talked about for years but had never been able to decide when to begin.

Steve did something lovely. He came up to me in the crowd at the wake, without saying anything, and he gently touched his forehead against mine.

Still in hiding

After the funeral Camilla and I went to stay at Rachel and Andy's house on a cliff overlooking the Pacific. I went up to the street to get something from my car and when I came back to the house Camilla was crying. 'Something terrible has happened.'

'Yeah, what?' I said apathetically.

Camilla had left one of the side doors open, and a draught had picked up Andy's large landscape painting and thrown it onto the arm of a wooden chair, ripping it open down the middle.

'That's not terrible,' I told her, looking at the canvas, sliced in two.

Antony still hadn't been found and I could feel the pressure mounting. I thought for sure he would have given himself up by now. As each day passed I became more and more frightened. When Camilla took the garbage up to the street and didn't return immediately I started to scream.

She had only stopped to sit on the steps behind the house to make a private phone call to her husband. I was beside myself. I was certain Antony had taken her. It was not logical. But my fear wasn't rational.

Adrenaline was coursing through my veins. I walked with Camilla up and down the beach three times a day to try to get rid of it.

The detective called to say there had been a sighting of Antony travelling to Melbourne and he wanted us to know that it would be in the paper the following day. We had no plans to buy a newspaper. We hadn't watched the television or bought a newspaper for ten days.

'When they find him they're not going to roll out the red carpet and the rose petals. People see people everywhere,' said the detective. 'He couldn't be in thirty different places in the one day.' I didn't know it at the time, but there had been eight hundred reported sightings of Antony. One person swore they saw him on the tube in London.

I told the detective, 'I don't feel safe.'

'You are safe,' he said firmly. 'Does that make you feel better?'

'A little,' I said, trying to make *him* feel better, but not believing my words.

I had noticed a large white van driving up and down the road behind the beach. I thought maybe there were plainclothes police in there, hot and bored, and laughing with one another. Were we under surveillance? Surely they could do it via satellite these days. I had just written a story about a woman who was under surveillance. We all know that life imitates fiction.

•

Camilla and I were still in hiding at the beach house when the time came for Nick's cremation. I had sent a car to pick up George, who was coming from the city, because I knew he wouldn't make it otherwise. He had been working on a building site and I knew he would be out at night, keeping company. He said he slept the whole way in the back seat. The driver took him to the wrong crematorium, and he only just made it, walking in as the service was beginning.

Ross and Margaret were there and Luke's uncle with his three children and Luke and two distant cousins of Nick's from the UK.

Patsy from the funeral home greeted us warmly, gave me a poem, and handed me a sprig of jacaranda her daughter had picked in the street that morning.

We stood in a circle around Nick's coffin and held hands. Luke's uncle was mumbling his prayers feverishly while clutching his daughter's hand. She was wearing the same dress she wore for the funeral, cut low at the front, her breasts exposed. Nick did not think women should display their good fortune in public. 'Not a good look,' I could hear him saying. He was probably laughing, laughing through his tears. He would not have liked the canned music though, and as I was looking for the speakers Patsy must have noticed the expression on my face because she turned it down.

Steve asked me if I wanted to read something. But I didn't have anything. I wished I had thought to grab the poetry book by Rumi from the apartment. It was the first book that Nick gave me, for Christmas in 1999, along with a miniature book of erotica. We hadn't loved each other

yet. Those books were our foreplay. I would have liked to read a particular poem of Rumi's. I did read it, one year later, at the laying of Nick's ashes:

In your light I learn how to love
In your beauty, how to make poems.
You dance inside my chest
Where no one sees you,
But sometimes I do,
And that sight becomes this art.

Steve said a prayer and kissed the coffin. We stood motionless as the sliding doors opened, and we watched the coffin move into the flames.

I had put my handbag on the ground in a corner and after the cremation I couldn't find my wallet. So distrustful was I of that family that I thought one of them had riffled through my bag and taken it. I wanted to laugh but it wasn't funny. My wallet turned up. I had left it at Rachel's house and I was ashamed of my paranoid thoughts. I put it down to the fact that we were still in hiding, and every day of those eighteen days when Antony had still not been found doubled the fear that ran through my veins. I couldn't stop myself from shaking. Nor could I eat or sleep. But my feeling that this family had secret aims were justified. The day before Antony was found Nick's lawyer called me on my mobile to say he was going to send Nick's will, asking for my email address. I said to him, 'But why do you have to send it so soon? Antony still hasn't been found.' He replied curtly, 'It's normal to send it out at this time.' I opened it on my laptop and learnt that Nick had

made me a co-executor along with Luke's uncle, and he had done everything he could to provide for George and me.

For the next two years Luke's uncle refused to give permission to release the original will in order to apply for probate. I was beyond caring really, but I thought that Nick's last will and testament should be honoured. Also, I saw this as another act of entitlement, and I hadn't forgotten Rachel's words when she first walked in the door: 'Nick was killed by entitlement.' I left it to the lawyers to try to execute the will. In the meantime I found a more positive occupation, a way to execute the other will Nick had left behind. I busied myself making a film based on his *Curator's Last Will and Testament*. That was God's irony.

•

Each day Camilla and I walked to the nearby Bible Garden. On a wooden table sat a clear plastic Tupperware container and inside it was a copy of the Holy Testament.

We sat at the table near a stone engraved with the Ten Commandments, and looked out to the lonely beach. Camilla counted the number of commandments that Antony had broken. I think she found four. We drank wine and listened to the menacing sounds of the helicopters overhead. The detective had told me that the police were searching for Antony's body among the rocks along the coast. I said, 'He's not dead. He's too much of a coward to be dead.'

It was one of the first questions Rachel had asked me: 'Do you feel he is alive?' In my bones, I knew he was alive. Just as on that fateful night when the police wouldn't give me a name, I knew that Nick was dead.

I opened the Bible at a random page and read from Matthew 5:44: 'But I say to you, who hear, love your enemies, do good to those who hate you.'

When I told Steve this later, he laughed. 'Yeah, well, if you don't love your enemies there aren't too many people left to love,' he said.

•

One evening, at about ten o'clock, we received a call. It was the detective. 'Antony has been found. I'm here with him. We found him in the bush near Upper Colo. I can't say anything more other than that he is well.'

Camilla asked the detective if he had a partner. She said, 'I love you, I love your wife and your children too.'

That night we played music for the first time. We turned it up to full volume and sat outside gazing at the dark waters of the ocean, and at the stars as they appeared between the clouds.

The next day we bought a newspaper. There was a photograph of Antony in the back seat of a car with his hands over his face. Ross Mellick called.

'Have you seen the paper?'

'Yes.'

'Have you seen the photo of Antony?'

'Yes.'

'I have a question to ask of you.'

'What's that?'

'Have you noticed anything odd?'

I spread out the paper on the floor of the living room, knelt down beside it and took another look. Antony was wearing a disposable forensic suit. 'No.'

'Take another look.'

'He has his hands over his face,' I said.

'Anything else?'

'He's covering it for the camera.'

'What's he wearing?'

'I don't know.'

'Well, they're not clothes. Take another look.'

'I don't know.'

'They're paper. He's wearing a paper suit.'

'So?'

'Don't you think that's sad?'

'No,' I said.

I called out to Camilla, who was in the kitchen, 'Camilla, do you think Antony's paper suit is sad?'

She called back, 'No sadder than the prison stripes he's going to be wearing for the rest of his life.'

PART TWO

The seeds of time

In the summer of 1999, Nick and I met up in Paris. He wanted to join me when I visited my friend Roland Topor's grave in the home of the muses in the cemetery in Montparnasse. We took a map from a man in the gatehouse and found Roland's plot in the corner with Baudelaire, Ionesco, Sartre, de Beauvoir and Soutine. It was marked with a small white tablet engraved with the words ROLAND TOPOR 1937–1997. There was a red geranium in a pot and a photo of Roland in a cracked glass frame. I placed a white rose on the grave, kissed my fingers and pushed them into the cold white gravel. We left the cemetery and joined a long line of people in a taxi queue near a huge stone fountain. The sun had just come out for the first time in four days. I took off my raincoat and a sudden gust of wind blew the water from the fountain sideways and drenched us both. Our clothes were soaked when we arrived at Gare du Nord to take the train to London.

•

'They'll love you,' said Nick as we stepped out of a London cab and walked through the gate of a brown-brick workers terrace, his mother's home in Battersea. I was excited. We were both so happy. My friends in Paris, our friends in London, were so happy too.

Nick had shown me a photograph of his mother, affectionately known as Baba.

'She has a lot of hair for an old woman,' I said.

Nick smiled kindly. 'It's a wig.'

I was introduced to a woman in a coiffured helmet in the style of Margaret Thatcher. Nick had mentioned his mother was a Thatcherite. Nick was a socialist. She never looked at me in the face directly. Her cold black eyes were fixed on me like a crow waiting for its prey, yet she didn't seem to see me. It was disconcerting. Nick was relaxed and took it all as a matter of course. We sat in the small, gloomy, over-furnished room, like so many other English living rooms, with royal-blue floral curtains, unnecessary tapestry cushions, green and violet porcelain parrots and images of pug dogs. Antony and Luke barely spoke. Chloe talked the most, mostly about their Christmas holidays the previous year, and the presents she had bought for her grandmother. She was nervous and trying to connect. I tried to match her face with her words.

I felt that Nick and I were in the wrong house with the wrong family. 'This can't be Nick's family,' I thought. It was a dream, a bad dream. I could feel the room fill with a fog—a fog of resentment. His mother asked me questions about my past. I could hear myself trying to compress ten, twenty, almost thirty years into a few sentences, but I felt as if I was telling someone else's story not my own. I was trying to put too many years into too few words, and the words were not enough. When I met Nick I had had the sense that I had already known him, and as his mother talked I noticed, on a table across the room, a photograph of Nick as a young man. His hair was black. I stared at that photograph. I never imagined that he would have had black hair. Of course he wouldn't have been born with grey hair, but it was a shock. It was also disconcerting because as a young man, he looked older—not nearly as open. His past went further back than mine. I was struck by a sudden realisation that he had lived so many years without me, and those were years I could never reach. That photograph pointed to a painful contradiction: a deep sense that I had known him before, and that there was an incommunicable past we would never be able to share.

I recalled our train journey from Paris to London. We had been seated facing the rear of the train, and as the train pulled out of the station and began its journey, we found ourselves literally travelling backwards, in reverse, with the green countryside flashing forward. That was how I felt in Nick's mother's living room too. We were physically going back into our own lives, and the out-of-focus world was falling away in front of us at enormous speed. I wanted to pick the train up with my fingers, like a toy, turn it around and put it back on the tracks so that I was travelling forward.

•

Nick called me a taxi. I was going to meet Rachel who was in London making a film. Nick was going to stay on for a while and join us later for dinner. When it was time to say goodbye I saw rigid faces. I looked for Antony. Nick said I might find him in the kitchen. I found him standing in the middle of the room, staring at his feet with his hands clenched at his sides. I said, 'Goodbye.' He didn't respond.

I was befuddled by the heat of this resentment, but far more upset about the wide gap between Nick's idea of how his family would behave and how they had actually treated me. Why were his ideas and reality so far apart?

•

I went back to the Chelsea Arts Club where Rachel was waiting for me in my room. I threw myself on the bed and burst into tears. I wept with my whole body. I couldn't stop. Nick arrived and we went out for dinner to the Groucho Club. Nick told Rachel how when he met me for the first time at the coffee shop near his work he had an erection during our entire one-hour meeting. Rachel laughed. We had fun. Nick and I were in love, and we forgot about his family.

•

I met Antony in a cafe on Kings Road. Even while drinking his beer, it struck me that he was playing a role; it seemed he was trying to be the person others thought he was. He told me he was attending an acting course. I knew of a good book on acting called *Impro*, and suggested Nick give it to Antony. Nick wrote an inscription inside it, adding: *with thanks to Juliet too.*

Nick told me that Antony went into a rage and demanded to know why on earth he should thank me. I thought that was an odd reaction, and way out of proportion, for a thirty-two-year-old man. Why not thank a person for a suggestion, for a thought, for a gift? For anything?

•

I saw Antony only a few other times over the next decade. We spent one Christmas Day together. Chloe seemed to be the centre of attention and I remember Antony and Luke giving her juicers and kitchen equipment. She opened them as if she didn't deserve them.

It was a very tense Christmas. By the time Luke turned up we had finished our lunch. He entered the dining room wearing a pair of swimming briefs, and holding a small bouquet of flowers in front of his crotch. Nick greeted him as if he was a long-lost prodigal son and sat at the table squeezing his hand.

Antony sat in silence. Nick and I drove him back to the city; in the car, when Nick asked him whether he was working, Antony said, 'I see no reason why I should work.' Then he said that he wanted to work as an actor but that someone else should have taught him how to act by now.

I was in the back seat and leant forward. 'But it's up to you to learn to act, isn't it?' He replied that he wasn't able to work because of all the things that had happened to him. I said, 'It's not what happens to you. It's what you do with what happens to you.' He didn't answer, or say any more to me after that.

•

The Waterlow beach house at Whale Beach had been a homey run-down cottage the family used for weekends and holidays. Then it had been rebuilt with the help of an architect who worked closely with Nick's first partner, and it was completed not long before she died. It was a very simple modern weatherboard house with a concave sloping roof that followed the steep line of the hill, and a bank of tall windows that looked out to the sea. But it was unfurnished and had no paintings or personal belongings in it: it didn't seem to be anyone's home.

The new house seemed to cast a spell on Nick as soon as he entered it. He became anxious and picked up tiny crumbs, wiped down already spotless stainless-steel benches and wandered through the rooms in a daze. It seemed to drain the life force, the spirit, out of him. And the minute he entered the house, he suddenly became controlling. For no reason at all, he began to line up objects, the glasses on shelves, to straighten the chairs around the table. I didn't like what this house did to Nick and nor did George, and he wasn't keen to spend time there.

•

Nick held a barbecue at the beach house for the workers of the 2000 Sydney Biennale. Afterwards I helped him clean up the house, and then we picked up George, who had been playing at a friend's house, and drove back to Sydney. Nick refused to take off his cooking apron before we left. I should never have let him drive as he had had a few drinks. In the car he kept saying, 'Everyone loves my house. They all loved my house.' I didn't realise how drunk he was until we stopped for petrol and, while he was filling up the car, he fell over by the pump. When he opened the passenger door to look for the steering wheel I told him, 'I'm driving from now on.'

•

Whale Beach was ruined by developers who pulled down trees to build monstrous weekenders the size of commercial buildings. The next-door neighbours tore out every tree and plant on their block in order to build a five-storey mansion with a swimming pool. When they insisted that the tiny angophora Nick planted be pulled out because one day it would ruin their view of the sea, Nick decided to sell. There were other reasons. He couldn't afford the land tax because the value of real estate had doubled in the ten years since he had bought it. He had to rent it out and he was always juggling to accommodate his tenants. But mainly he was worried that Antony would burn it down while tenants were in it. Luke and Chloe didn't want to sell the house. However, Antony said he understood that Nick couldn't afford to keep it and supported Nick's decision to sell it. Before the exchange of contracts took place, Nick invited Antony to choose any books he wanted from the house. Nick told me Antony chose only one and when Nick came into the room he quickly turned it over so Nick wouldn't see the title. But Nick had seen it out of the corner of his eye. It was a book about death.

I asked Nick, 'What do you make of that?' He didn't say anything. Perhaps he thought the unthinkable, as I did: that it could be read as a sign his son might be contemplating taking his own life.

•

The day before settlement I was at the house helping Nick to pack up. When he said that Antony was coming to the house for lunch the following day, I took all the kitchen knives out of the drawers, wrapped them in a beach towel and hid them under a bush in the backyard.

'Just to be on the safe side,' I told Nick.

I wasn't there for the lunch but Nick told me that Antony went into a violent rage: he and Luke had fought and managed to put a hole right through the living room wall. Their prawns were left untouched on the table. Luke told me later that Nick didn't want Antony to go to the house for lunch that day but Luke had insisted and he regretted that.

The police were called and by the time they arrived Antony had calmed down. They asked Antony if he had anger issues and Antony said, 'Yes I do.' The police left and Antony wasn't charged.

•

Antony had been invited to the baptism of Chloe and Ben's first child. He chose to read a passage from *The Prophet* by Kahlil Gibran. I can't recall the words but I remember that as he read Antony kept looking across the room accusingly at Nick. Chloe was rolling her eyes. Luke sat in silence, his face redder than usual. The ceremony took place in a room under St Canice's church. On that summer's day the heat was oppressive and we were all fanning ourselves with whatever we could find. Nick told me afterwards how uncomfortable he felt during the reading. Although Nick was interested in mysticism and had many books in his library on the subject, I knew that he didn't have much time for Gibran, so when I found *The Prophet* among the books on his bedside table after he died, I thought, 'Was he still trying to understand and find a way to connect with Antony?'

After the baptism we all went to Bronte Park for a picnic. The guests were chatting and eating around a table and Antony and Luke were standing apart from the rest, talking amicably under a fig tree.

•

George and I attended Chloe and Ben's wedding. At the reception, I sat at the table next to Nick with family friends.

Nick stood to speak. He began by acknowledging the Gadigal people, the traditional owners of the land. He continued:

I was in Melbourne last night for the opening of *For Matthew and Others*, an exhibition that celebrates the lives and art of many people living with mental illness. It reminded me of how no family is untouched; and that makes today even more memorable for me, as Chloe's father, for our family, for our loved ones and all our friends, both those present and those in many parts of the globe who would wish to be here. One who I feel is here in spirit is Chloe's mother Romy, who would have been overjoyed by today's ceremony. Love is in the air and nothing is more fragrant. And how times change: not so very long ago today's ceremony would not have been possible in a Catholic church—mind you, Father Steve Sinn, who has been a wonderful friend and support to me and whom I regard as one of Australia's true spiritual leaders, always manages to find a humane rather than doctrinaire response, and he appreciates the views of others.

Nick made us all laugh when he described his struggle, in the plane back from Melbourne, to remove the top of the long-life milk container for his tea, and how he managed to squirt it into the face of a woman seated next to him. He mentioned how Ben and Chloe first met and that the most important thing for him was not whether Ben and Chloe would marry but whether Ben truly and deeply loved his daughter, and that he would care for her in all the ways Nick would wish. Then he mentioned Antony. 'It is sad for me, Chloe and Luke that Antony isn't here today, and I send him our love and our support.' He went on to describe at length Antony's long struggle with mental illness. It was the first time I had heard him mention his son's illness openly and in public.

'Today's vows are there for life, and to see love prevail here, and so positively alter two people's lives, renews faith in a world that is full of wonder and surprises,' he said. He lifted his glass. 'To my daughter Chloe and Ben, I give you my love, my support and my wishes for a long and fully lived life together.'

When he had finished, some of the younger guests, friends of the groom who did not know Nick, came up to him and thanked him for talking so openly about a subject that was still taboo, especially at a wedding. Despite Nick's heartbreaking speech the family friends at our table made toasts to Chloe's mother, but none said a word about Antony's illness, or how Nick had expressed his sorrow in his speech. I was forcing back tears. That was when I realised how deeply affected Nick was by his son's illness. But the code of silence that prevailed at that table was, to me, just as heartbreaking as Nick's speech.

I don't know what George thought of it. He was eighteen. He got very drunk and danced intimately with a few of the older women.

I went outside onto the verandah and stared for a long time at the dark forms of two hundred-year-old bunya trees, and I prayed for the spirit of those gigantic trees to enter my being.

•

I have so many questions for Nick. But I asked them of him when he was alive and he didn't answer them then. His mother put down her only child, but she didn't seem to be aware of it. A cousin said, 'She's depressed. Wouldn't you be after what she's been through?' The last time I stayed with her, in 2005, she spent the day with her friend, the ballet dancer Donald MacLeary, in her bedroom. Nick saw me halfway up the stairs, listening. He told me how much it had annoyed him to have travelled all the way from Australia to London especially to see his mother and then to find she had invited Donald to stay.

I bristled at Nick's mother's humiliating remarks to her son. Someone would say, 'I like your shoes, Nick.' She would totter over to Nick, look at his feet disdainfully, and say, 'I'm glad *you* like them.' When Nick was awarded the Medal of the Order of Australia for service to the arts his mother said, 'Well, there's hope for all of us.' Eventually I refused to stay in her house when we were in London. She didn't like that.

When we met, one of the first things Nick told me was that his children didn't support him. He told me they didn't understand his work. They seemed to resent him.

I thought it was wrong that he should accept this, and we discussed it a lot. Perhaps he could do nothing about it?

Early on we had lunch in a restaurant with his children, and my nephew came with us. Antony was an hour and a half late, claiming he couldn't find the restaurant. I found it irritating that Nick didn't seem to mind at all, even though he used to repeat to me in our early days: 'No more Mr Nice Guy.'

Nick told me it was Antony to whom he felt closest, with whom he could talk. This may have been why Nick was never going to give up on that possibility. Maybe he thought he would always be able to talk Antony round. Or perhaps there was a hidden bond between them. Nick's children found it hard to accept his relationship with me and my son. Eventually I stopped asking Nick about them. Once he entered the door of our apartment, he seldom mentioned them.

•

After my first argument with Antony I was so terrified that I didn't want him to be near my son. He did visit a few times early on; George remembers meeting him in the kitchen.

I felt George and I were both people to be envied by Antony. Envy was something I could smell. I could taste it. I could feel its danger.

Nick's love

I asked Nick often, while lying beside him, our toes touching:
'How is it you can be so very loving? Your mother is so
unkind. She's always putting you down, shaming you.'

'But you've only seen that side of her. There are other
sides to her,' he said.

'She's had plenty of opportunity to show them to me,
and she never has,' I said. 'Did you always love?'

'Yes.'

'But did you always like yourself?'

'Yes,' said Nick. 'I always felt confident. Something
within told me I could love. I knew it, always.'

He told me he felt loved by his nanny, his cousins and
some teachers at school. He said that he felt he was lucky
to have been sent away to a boarding school at the age of
six because it taught him to be independent and helped
him to look outward. I thought that the way Nick loved
could only have been sown by the seeds of adversity. He

had the spirit of a poet. It was a love that came from the stars—from God. As Wart said, 'Nick loved supremely.' His love was like a wind that picked you up and rose higher than the trees. He found it, and then he abandoned himself to it, losing himself to it. And then he gave endlessly, selflessly, to others. When he looked at a work of art he put himself aside, unconscious, as it were, of himself. I think this was what gave him a deep understanding of artists. He had the deep humility an artist has to have in order to create something true. He understood the necessity of continually renewing innocence and he treasured his sense of wonder. Perhaps it was easier for him—as it is for us all—to see the truth in art than in life. I was often surprised to see how in his life he gave himself to people who weren't his supporters, to those who didn't necessarily love him. He truly was able to follow the teachings of Jesus and 'love your enemies'.

•

After Nick's death I received an email from a friend of his: *We are so sorry about this completely avoidable tragedy.*

Was it avoidable? There had been no end of red flags, as the detective had said. Every time I saw a police car a fear would rise in my chest. I spent so many evenings lying awake, waiting for Nick to return, with my breath caught in my throat, listening to sirens or, on occasions, helicopters hovering over the nearby park. And some nights I even felt the presence of someone, I felt it might have been Antony, watching our apartment.

Those murders could well have happened at the beach house, two years earlier, the day after I hid all the kitchen knives in the garden. Or at Antony's house in Stanmore when he said to Luke, 'I have no choice but to kill you all.' Or the afternoon at Colo Heights when he pointed to his hut and told Nick and Luke, 'That is the torture chamber.'

A relative who used to visit the family when Antony was a child told me that Antony could do anything he wanted and get away with it. A neighbour scoffed, 'He was the golden boy.' A cousin who knew the children while they were still at home said that Antony was always in opposition, always testing his limits, but still he was never given boundaries. He was allowed to do anything. Perhaps he was always uncontrollable. Friends who had Antony to stay in America when he was around twenty wrote to his mother to say that he was not well. Nick had expressed his concern about his son's violence and his partner had said that it was normal, that children fight, and that her brothers had always fought. Antony's mother knew her son was violent and unstable, but she must have had a lot of faith in him because, as I discovered when going through Nick's papers after his death, she had made him an executor of her will.

•

It wasn't long after Nick had witnessed Antony punching a hole in the wall of their beach house that he told me he wanted to allow Antony to have his mail sent to our street address. I refused. We argued about it. I told Nick that it would just give Antony an excuse to accuse me of tampering with his letters, of opening them, or hiding them, or stealing the contents. I knew Antony was both paranoid and violent. Letters addressed to Antony started to arrive, and I returned them at once to the sender. Eventually they stopped coming.

Nick told me that he took Antony to see a psychologist when Antony had said that Nick should find him a job and a place to live. The psychologist pointed out to Antony that he was forty years old. He snapped at her, 'What has age got to do with it?' He told the psychologist that his stepmother had friends in the film industry who should have taught him how to act by now. When Nick told me this I said, 'Please do not mention my friends' names, my name or my son's to Antony ever again. I don't want our names in his head.'

I found a note in Nick's handwriting referring to that meeting: *Do not pathologise Antony.* Was this what the psychologist had advised? Only after the trial, when I was sent Antony's medical records, did I realise how much effort Nick and Chloe and others had gone to in order to have Antony scheduled. Yet despite a ten-year history of violence, the death threats made to both Nick and Chloe, and Antony's paranoid behaviour and thinking, the doctors continually resisted enforced scheduling and medication. Their reason was that Antony was 'not at imminent risk'.

Losing one's senses

The family was hobbled together—and they were floundering. Luke kept up his communication with Antony until Antony took out an apprehended violence order against him. Despite many warnings and her husband's requests, Chloe refused to break her ties with Antony. And Nick was never going to abandon any of his children. Dinners were arranged at Antony's place a number of times and then aborted. Nick had confided to Wart how frightened he was. But he never told me.

On the night of one such dinner Nick called me from his mobile to say that Chloe and Ben had turned around and were going home because Antony wouldn't allow Ben to be there, and Chloe wouldn't go to the dinner without Ben. Nick was in the street in Stanmore outside Antony's flat. I had already advised Nick to eat beforehand, and not to touch any food Antony had prepared. Now I told Nick to get back in his car and drive home. Then I sat up in bed, frozen, and waited for him to return—with the same cold dread that I would feel while waiting for the police to arrive on the night of Nick's death.

•

At the funeral Nick's GP told me that she had warned Nick many times that Antony was dangerous. I paid a couple of visits to a psychologist whom Nick had seen. She told me that the two of them had discussed ways in which he could protect himself from Antony. She said Nick had told her how frightened he was and so she found it baffling that he had taken Antony in his car to Chloe's house. Chloe and Nick must have had a plan cooked up between them. I found many diary entries mentioning meetings with Antony at a coffee shop. Beside Antony's name was a dollar sign, and beside that, an exclamation mark. *Antony $!*

•

A few months before Nick's death, he began to behave more erratically. He no longer felt safe in the dark. He was jumpy. Perhaps he no longer had the resources to trust his instincts; maybe he had pushed fear aside to such a deep place, and for so long, that it had become part of his daily life, and he couldn't see it or feel it anymore. The psychologist had told me that Nick was less anxious after seeing her for a few sessions. I asked her how she could tell. She said, 'He filled out a questionnaire.' Do questionnaires encourage people to be honest? I think they do the opposite. How does a person who wants to please, who has spent their life trying to help others, answer those questions? A questionnaire offers a range of choices that are 'either/or' when they should be 'both/and'. Also, one can tick the box 'mildly anxious' and ten minutes later, when outside the comfort of a quiet room, it is possible for that answer to change to 'very anxious'. I told her, 'No. Nick was becoming more and more anxious at that time.' So Nick, too, presented himself well, in front of the psychologist.

Antony's medical notes from St Vincent's stated that Antony always presented well. Despite appeals to the hospital, on average once a month from 2006 to 2007 by family members and others—their notes recorded paranoid psychosis and a history of violent behaviour, including death threats, a rape charge, verbal threats and threats with a knife to both Nick and Chloe—the doctors did not recommend scheduling. They recommended antipsychotic drugs but left the decision of whether or not to take them up to Antony, who refused. Until I was given Antony's medical history, I thought Nick had not done enough, but I see now that he did all he could have. Those records show a failure of our world.

I found a note in Nick's papers with these words underlined from the book *Surviving Schizophrenia*:

The data on the effectiveness of drugs are so clear that any physician or psychiatrist who fails to try them on a person with schizophrenia is probably incompetent. It is not that drugs are the only ingredients necessary to treat schizophrenia successfully; they are just the most essential ingredient. They are most effective at reducing delusions, and aggressive or bizarre behaviour.

Also underlined is: 'What then is the proper role for insight-oriented psychotherapy in the treatment of schizophrenia? It has none, and should be explicitly avoided.'

I found letters to Antony:

Dearest Antony,

I find it hard to say things when we are together, and particularly recently when we always seem to end up being in conflict. I hope that by writing I can find a way of bringing us closer together, because I do feel for you enormously. I love you very much and I want to help you now in any way I can.

One problem is I don't know exactly how to help. I have discussed schizophrenia with various people whose children suffer from it, and most say that the really important thing a parent can do is to be there and act as a safety net and try not to take personally the anger and frustration that is often vented at them. I want you to know that no matter what happens, or if you decide, as you have, to assign guardianship to someone else, I will always be there for you. And, if there is something in particular that you need, emotionally or practically, please ask, and I will do to the best of my ability whatever I can to help you.

Almost everyone I have spoken to has advised that it is much harder to function and lead a reasonable life and do work without some form of medication. I have been enormously upset to see you suffering, and I now am trying to understand that your anger towards me is a part of this condition . . . Please let me know if you would like me to help.

With all my love, Dad

I found Nick's instructions and notes to himself regarding Antony and his mother:

I feel deeply for you, also for Baba.

Do you believe there is nothing wrong with you? I believe there is.

I can't give you the help you need most, psychiatric and medical.

Think of my needs and boundaries. I will listen and try not to interrupt. I will be myself, be direct, be honest. I will have no expectations. I cannot help you. I cannot make you take medication. I can only tell you what I think. I cannot help you to help yourself. I cannot live your life. I understand what you think and believe . . . but I believe that . . .

I can't take on someone else's fate/reality. We are separate beings and I can't control your life. Be warm and kind. Know the difference between the well and the ill Antony. Understand when it is the illness talking. I wish you would take medication and keep seeing me or/and the psychiatrist.

The arraignment

On the way to the courthouse, at Steve's suggestion, he, Luke and I ducked into St Mary's Cathedral. I lit a candle for Nick and put my hands together. Every image, sound, taste, footfall was a prayer for Nick. I had lit so many candles. I needed the light.

We were led into the empty courtroom and the witness support pointed out the open dock where Antony would sit. She suggested we sit on the far side of the room but Luke wanted to sit in the aisle, close to the dock, where he would have a clear view of Antony and, more importantly, Antony would be able to see him. I sat on the other side of Steve. We heard some shouting outside the courthouse, and a policeman entered and apologised to the judge and asked for more time. A few minutes later a handcuffed Antony was led into the dock. Wearing a slightly too big white collared shirt, he sat with the same rigid body and impassive robotic gaze that I had always known him to have; he stared straight ahead, or at the judge when spoken to. Steve, Luke and I fixed our gazes on Antony but he never once looked our way. Steve turned to me and said, 'The worst thing of all is not being able to love.' I remembered the line from Dostoevsky's *The Brothers Karamazov*: 'Fathers and teachers, I ponder, "What is hell?" I maintain that it is the suffering of being unable to love.'

Antony was asked to stand. The judge asked him, 'Do you plead guilty or not guilty to the murder of Chloe Waterlow?'

'Not guilty.'

'Do you plead guilty or not guilty to the murder of Nick Waterlow?'

'Not guilty.'

Antony was led out and the arraignment was over.

We filed out of the courtroom and talked in the foyer. The witness support asked me how I thought Antony looked and I told her, 'Just the same.'

Yvonne, Nick's personal assistant at COFA, said, 'He's the same old Antony, just a little greyer in front, that's all.'

Luke was upset because Antony never once looked at him. He was surrounded by a group of old school friends, telling them he should be able to visit his brother. He wanted to know why he couldn't visit Antony in jail. The witness support explained that he couldn't because he'd made a statement and he might be called up as a witness at the trial. But Luke said, 'There won't be a proper trial. Antony is paying for his medical reports. The decision will be made by a judge.'

'Has Antony ever shown you empathy?' I asked Luke.

'No.'

'So why do you want to see him when you know he has no empathy?'

'He's my brother; we will always have a relationship. I want to tell him I'm having a baby. Bruce has been to see him. He thinks I should see him.'

'Who is Bruce?' I demanded.

'The headmaster of Luke and Antony's school,' said Steve quietly, indicating a man in the group around Luke.

'What do you think, Bruce? Should I be able to see Antony?' asked Luke.

'It would be the Christian thing to do. I think it would do you and Antony good,' Bruce replied. 'There is the law, and there is the Christian thinking.'

I looked at Bruce and thought, 'Who is this guy?'

We had lunch at the court cafe and I sat next to Bruce, who said to Luke, 'Remember, Antony is drugged and he is suffering from depression.'

I leant his way. 'He might just be a coward.'

Bruce thought for a moment and said, 'Yes.'

I asked Luke what he thought he would achieve by seeing Antony. Luke didn't answer straight away. Then he said, 'He's my brother. I want to ask Antony why he did what he did.'

I looked up at an imaginary brick wall, and Bruce and Luke followed my gaze, puzzled. 'It is like trying to ask a brick wall to give you a hug,' I said. 'It won't happen.' I reminded Luke about the emails Antony had sent him.

'Yes, but that was years ago,' he said.

'It was only two years ago.'

In one email to Luke Antony wrote: *I have been torturing you for years and you are too stupid to realise it.*

Steve said, 'Why do you want to give him that power?'

Luke talked a lot and told us all how Antony, when he was young, threw his mother on the couch and smashed up things at home.

'You don't throw your mother onto the couch,' said Steve. 'Antony should have been pulled up at the age of twelve.'

Luke told us how Antony refused to join his mother on her last holiday, but when she died he was howling in the hospital. 'And now,' said Luke, 'all he wants from the estate is our mother's roll-top desk and papers.' Luke looked at me. 'How was your relationship with Dad?'

Luke had asked me this question before. 'It was harmonious and loving. We had a lot in common. There were a few tiffs but not many and they usually involved a night on the sofa, and once or twice in a hotel room; and they were always about the same thing—his family. But we laughed, all the time, at everything. Your dad had the most wonderful sense of the ridiculous.'

'You have that too,' said Steve.

'Yes, but it's not the same when you can't share it.'

On the television that night there was a short segment about the arraignment. I heard the reporter's voiceover say that Antony had fought a long battle with schizophrenia and I turned it off. 'He has fought no battle with that illness,' I thought. 'He is a psychopath who has no empathy. If they keep Antony in a hospital and give him drugs and then let him out he will kill again. I know it. We all know it now. I know how long he has held on to his resentment

towards his father and Chloe. I saw it in his fists when I
first met him.'

•

Luke called me to arrange a meeting to discuss his father's
will. I said I wanted to meet in a quiet place, and he
suggested the cemetery. I visualised the bleak treeless
cemetery at Vaucluse, on the edge of the headland.

'Luke. I don't want to meet in the cemetery.'

We chose a busy restaurant by the beach. It was a little
noisy, but the crowds offered a kind of protection and
allowed us to talk in private.

Luke and I sat by the window, and from the table I could
see a bride in white and a groom in black tie cavorting
near the waves for a cameraman. In the foreground, closer
to us, another man in a black suit, maybe the chauffeur,
was watching them, twirling a golf umbrella like a baton.

The young waitress was trying to take our orders, and
Luke, the menu in his hand, was cross-examining her as
if she was in a witness stand.

'How is it done?'

'What do you mean?'

'How is it prepared?'

'It is lightly pan-fried and served on a bed of peas. It's
very nice.'

'Light?'

'Yes.'

'What does it taste like?'

'Well, it's a white fish, firm.'

'Is it nice?'

'Very nice.'

'Is it better than the chicken?'

'They're both good,' she said patiently.

'The chicken is a bit rich, eh?'

'Not really.'

'What about the sticky date? Which is better, the sticky date or the cheesecake?'

'It depends what you like.'

'I know sticky date. I'll try the cheesecake. Is it good?'

Luke saw me smiling and said, 'It has always been hard for me to trust.'

I went to the bathroom and when I returned to the table I asked Luke, 'Maybe you didn't trust your dad? Or his relationship with me?'

In the bathroom, all at once, it had occurred to me that 'trust', or lack of it, was at the heart of this family's problems. There had always been a lack of trust. No one trusted. But Nick and Chloe were dead because they both trusted Antony well beyond his power. They expected of Antony what he could not see or hear.

A plump woman in a short black dress and very high heels tottered past the window—a surreal outfit for the beach. In the restaurant the men were underdressed, in thongs and shorts and T-shirts, and the women were dressed as if for a night out on the town, with plunging necklines and high heels, and too much make-up and jewellery. It added to the unreality of the time.

I asked Luke where his share of his father's ashes was now. Nick's ashes had been divided between Luke and me. I wasn't sure who had decided this. When I asked Patsy from the funeral home, she said, 'That's the way we do things these days because people in families want to do things differently.' Luke told me that one afternoon some guy from the funeral home had turned up outside his door in a tiny car, handed him a cardboard box and said, 'Here's your dad.'

He told me that he had already taken some of Nick's ashes to Nick's mother in London, where she kept them in an urn at her house. She had asked for them. Some had been scattered at Portman Square, and also under a tree at Nick's second cousin's house in the country.

Luke said he wanted to bury some at COFA and also some at his mother's grave.

I told him I would like 'my half' to be placed in a niche at St Canice's church.

It was dark when we left the cafe. We walked for a while by the water then, without saying anything, Luke headed off into the park. I called out, 'I'm going to my car.' I watched Luke walk away under the trees and thought, 'He has lost his entire family. His mother, his father, his sister, and in a way his brother too. Only his grandmother is alive.'

PART THREE

Let me weep forever

I told Steve that I was organising a recital at our home and he offered to bless the apartment at the same time. A crowd of forty or more pushed their way into the corridor and living rooms.

I watched Steve carefully sprinkle the blue front door with holy water and thought, 'What a wonderful act—to bless a front door.' For years I used to leave it open. Now that door is always locked, and when I returned to the apartment, the first thing I did was have a video camera installed downstairs. The day after it was installed someone rang the buzzer. I crept up to the monitor, and when I saw the image of a man I didn't recognise, I was terrified. He went away. It wasn't logical but I was convinced he was hiding in the hallway and I called my friend Meera, who had a set of keys. She offered to come by and check the hallways to make sure he had gone. Later I found out he was a builder working in another apartment and only wanted access to the fire-alarm system.

Steve blessed the bathroom, the bedroom and the kitchen with holy water and he asked my friend's children to read the blessings. The singer Gemma couldn't look at me as she sang the lament 'O Let Me Weep' from Purcell's *The Fairy Queen*. She said later that it had been one of the hardest things she had ever had to do. David Malouf saw her hands shaking and held up the music for her as she sang:

> *O let me weep, for ever weep,*
> *My eyes no more shall welcome sleep;*
> *I'll hide me from the sight of day,*
> *And sigh my soul away.*
> *He's gone, he's gone, his loss deplore;*
> *And I shall never see him more.*

When she finished, the crowd in the room was silent. A long time passed before anyone said anything. The Dean of COFA was glancing at me furtively, his head hung low. Steve told me he found the lyrics very confronting.

'He's gone,' I told Steve. 'Those are the words that need to be sung.'

'I never did like those bereavement cards that read, *Death is nothing at all. I have only slipped away into the next room*,' said Steve.

The trial

The week before Antony's trial, I was invited to meet with the prosecution lawyer. I was taken through bulletproof glass doors into his office, where a small man greeted me with a smile; a smile that offended me enormously, and I wasn't able to return it graciously. 'This is about a double murder,' I thought. 'What is there to smile about?' The homicide detective was there with the witness support, and another prosecution lawyer. They told me that Antony's lawyers and the prosecution lawyers had agreed that Antony was mentally ill at the time of the offence and he would be given a verdict of 'not guilty due to mental illness'. The trial would take a day or two at most. I was stunned, as I had been mentally preparing for a three-week murder trial.

'But he was violent,' I said.

'Yes, but that was due to the illness,' said the still-smiling prosecution lawyer.

•

I had bought a leather biker jacket to wear for the trial; it was inspired by a young woman who slept in an alcove on a piece of cardboard near the entrance to the Cité Internationale des Arts in Paris. I watched her sleep in her leather jacket and what looked to me like a pair of ski boots with sharp steel studs all over them. I wanted her boots too.

•

On the morning of the trial, Jane arrived with a pink camellia she had picked in the street. Then Sally Bongers, Rachel and Kate arrived. Rachel wanted a shower. I gave her a towel and she undressed, stepped into the glass recess and turned to me.

'Do you like my breasts?'

'They're beautiful. Nick would have liked them too,' I thought.

Jane slapped the camellia onto my photocopier with a page from the Rumi book and made black and white copies for each of us; creating, in a second, a mysterious and poetic image: the type among shadowed creases, black elliptical forms of the leaves dark as stone, negative on the page, and a delicate bright three-dimensional white flower with each stamen intact. We stood in a circle by the piano holding hands, and each of us in turn read a line from the Rumi poem.

Jane drove us slowly and carefully to the courthouse. It was a trial by judge alone. Luke was sitting behind the dock with his uncle and friends. We sat in the back row. Antony was brought up to the dock where he sat rigidly with his back to us. He pleaded 'not guilty' to the murders and was taken away again. We went into a waiting room and the prosecution lawyer asked Luke and me whether we would agree to let Antony make a statement. He told us that Antony would read it but only on the condition that he was not cross-examined. Luke's uncle said, 'It's up to you Luke.' Luke walked over to me and asked me what I thought. I questioned the lawyer, 'Do you want to cross-examine him?'

He said, 'No.'

'Well, why not let him make the statement then,' I said to Luke. I was interested to hear what he had to say for himself. Luke agreed. We went back into the courtroom. Antony's lawyer walked over to the dock and spoke to him. Then Antony took out a piece of paper, unfolded it and read.

'Never in my wildest dreams did I imagine I would kill Chloe and Dad but I did. It was me and that is what I have to live with. I miss my family incredibly.'

I didn't believe a word he said. Antony didn't even mention that he had grievously harmed Chloe and Ben's child.

We were each given an abbreviated copy of the Crown case. The orders sought by the Crown were that Antony be found not guilty of the charges by reason of mental illness. The trial was adjourned. On the second and final day of the trial, Jane and Sally and I arrived at the court. Steve was there too. He sat next to me and I gave him a copy of the Crown case, which he read while the judge was talking. When Steve finished reading he leant forward and put his face in his hands. I debated whether to comfort him or help him in some way but I decided against it. I felt it wasn't my right.

The prosecution lawyer remarked to the judge that in Antony's statement he did not even mention Chloe's daughter whose throat he had cut on the night. She had survived but would be scarred forever. The judge told us he was convinced that Antony had shown remorse for his actions, and this statement was printed widely in the papers that evening. The judge pronounced Antony not guilty due to mental illness and a woman in the front row clapped. Antony's lawyers went up to the dock and shook his hand. They were behaving as if they had won a battle and there had been a chance of another outcome. But as Luke had predicted at the arraignment, the verdict had been decided long beforehand.

Steve, Jane and I left the courthouse and walked towards a barrage of cameras and microphones. We had decided not to speak to the press but at the last minute Jane stopped in front of the cameras. 'There is a gap in our system. Nick and Chloe died because there was no protection given by mental health services. They died because Antony couldn't be scheduled. There has to be a review, so people who can't see the point in taking their medication can be scheduled, so members of their family don't have to be killed.'

We went to a coffee shop behind the courthouse and talked about the trial. Sally arrived; she was tearful and kept repeating that her sister who was a psychiatrist could have scheduled Antony if only she had seen him. 'Stop saying that,' I said. 'She couldn't have. All the other doctors who had actually seen him didn't, or they couldn't.'

Grief

After the deaths, a work colleague and friend of Nick's invited me for dinner with him and his wife. At the table he said coyly, 'It might just have been me, but I felt there was a lot of anger at Nick's funeral.'

I looked at him with disbelief. 'Just you? No one else? Not the other two thousand people there?' Steve had delivered one of the angriest homilies I had ever heard, I told him. 'We were all angry. Why wouldn't we be? The gentlest, most loving man had been slaughtered by his son, with his daughter, the mother of his grandchildren, and with the children as witnesses.' I told him that detectives were in the crowd and I had been in hiding, and in fear for my life and that of my son. Luke had been in hiding in the country. 'It must have been in the papers,' I said. 'Antony had not been found. We could hardly breathe for fear.'

'Oh, I didn't know,' he said. He leant forward. 'There's only one thing I regret.'

'What's that?' I asked him.

'I'm sorry that I never got to show Nick my paintings.'

'That's all you regret?' I looked at him, astonished.

And he was astonished at the fury in my face.

I have heard so many times since that anger is not necessary. 'Not pretty,' said Luke's uncle who was sitting in Nick's office chair. As co-executors of Nick's will we were there to meet a field officer from the Mitchell Library who was taking a look at Nick's papers. When is it acceptable to be angry? My uncle warned me to 'watch out for anger because it leads to bitterness and that can stifle creativity'. I fired back an angrier email saying that I thought that for artists anger was the very source of creativity, although it may never reveal itself in the finished work: Lucian Freud said that his anger didn't show in his paintings but that as a man he was filled with anger and indignation. A gallery director told me, 'But there's no anger in Picasso's work.' What about *Guernica*? Anger is the source of much of my poetry and people never recognise it because, by the time they read, it is transformed.

Anyway, who wouldn't be angry when a man murders two people and doesn't even get a slap on the wrist for it?

•

The victim's homicide support group gave me a list of psychologists to call. I scanned the pages trying to work out, by their names, which one would be the most helpful. I couldn't tell so I turned to their addresses and called one who was close by. She picked up the phone.

'So, it's some kind of domestic violence . . .' she said.

I told her what had happened.

'Oh, I went to that funeral.'

'Did you know Nick?'

'Yes. I met him. I had dinner with him once. I don't have a problem with that, do you?'

'Well, I'm not sure,' I said. 'I'll have to think about it.'

'I didn't know him intimately or anything,' she reassured me.

I made an appointment with her and then I went down to the beach to think more about it. 'I can't possibly see this woman,' I thought. I was most disturbed by her initial presumption: 'So, it's some kind of domestic violence.' I rang her back and cancelled. Then I rang the victim's support group and complained.

They sent me to another counsellor, this time a specialist in homicide matters. I had just had lunch with the son of a distant cousin of Nick's; he had waited until the bill came to tell me the reason why he wanted to meet me. He said that he'd had a message from Baba in the UK. She wanted me to send her Nick's paintings. He said, 'She says they belong to her.' By the time I walked into the counsellor's rooms, a little late, I was flustered and hot with anger. I felt I was bringing into her room a great ball of fire.

Maybe she was used to that and this was the reason she was wearing a protective white dust jacket and the wrong glasses. We sat opposite one another and she said, 'If I am looking at you strangely it is because I have the wrong glasses on and I cannot see you properly.' I spent the next few minutes debating with myself if it really should matter whether or not she could see me. I decided it was probably a good thing that she couldn't—for her at least. My face must have been twisted like a rag. She told me that Nick was let down by the medical system. And that the doctors should have picked up Antony's mental problems earlier and done something about it. She was the fifth medical worker to tell me that. She lent me a handbook on grief which I read and returned by mail.

Nick's last moments replayed over and over in my head when I went to bed at night, and again each morning when I woke. After six months the images began to grow less and less distinct. They appeared again only when someone waved a knife around absent-mindedly while telling an anecdote in their kitchen, or when I saw a cheese knife on a plate, or if I passed a knife shop.

I had quotes stuck up all over my apartment, but after Nick died I threw a lot of them away. I needed a new set of quotes. But I kept the one from the Book of Job: *If you set your heart aright you will lie down and none can make you afraid.* I liked those words, 'set your heart'; I liked to think I could set my heart, and of course I would have to continually reset it. I stuck another quote on the edge of the fridge door, so I could read it each time I reached for the milk: *For it is blind and fatal to trust men beyond their power and to expect of them what they cannot and will not hear.* Next to it I put up another: *One is born. The rest of life is not certain in the slightest.* As if I needed reminding. But I did—all day long. And one more, the most important, the main one: *It takes no great effort to imagine the fanciful. What is needed is the ability to imagine the real.*

•

While I was in the queue at the post office, the detective called me on my mobile to tell me he was happy for me to have Nick's pocket diary. 'But as there are fluids on it, I think it's best to give you a photocopy.' I was at the counter buying a stamp to send a letter to a friend of Nick's in New York. I turned and made my way to the door. I started to breathe heavily, as if gasping for air, as if I was suddenly underwater. The detective didn't say anything. Once I was outside I started to sob.

'Where are you?' he said.

'I'm in the street.'

'I'll come over now and we'll have a coffee,' he said.

'I am so frightened.'

'If there is one word you would use to describe your fear, what would it be?' he asked gently.

I thought for a minute. 'Resentment,' I said. I told the detective I was upset that Nick's mother wouldn't allow me to attend Nick's memorial service in London.

He said, 'But you don't have to have anything to do with her, do you?'

I went to a wine bar with a young Australian artist and his mother, a woman with a fragile face, who had come to visit him. Almost straight away she confided in me that she was probably a little bit like Nick: that she had had a very domineering and over-involved mother, and had found it hard to make decisions in her life. She said that her eldest son had told her recently: 'Mum, you are still trying to please people.' She said that she had no boundaries, and added that she had spent her whole life trying to find a way to live with this disability. 'We need boundaries,' she said firmly. 'As people, we aren't evolved enough to be able to live without them.'

I had only just met her and I was taken aback by her admission, and she didn't know Nick but she had already divined his relationship with his mother just from the news in the papers of the tragic events. What is it like to be the son of a mother who won't let you go?

It had been hard for me to let my son George go. When he finished school at eighteen, he started to party hard and sleep during the day. He applied half-heartedly for jobs, and was always let go. I was worried about his behaviour, and I would wait up for him, often until the early hours of the morning. One night, I overheard George and his friends having a philosophical conversation in his bedroom. It was late and they had been drinking and their words were slurred. George said, 'Mum leaves twenty bucks on the sideboard for me every day.' There was a long pause. Then one of his friends responded, 'Well, you don't have to take it, do you?' There was another, longer pause, and I heard George's voice again. 'Would you leave twenty bucks on the counter if you saw it there?'

That was when I realised that I was doing my son actual harm by giving him what I considered to be sandwich money. Also, what was I doing spying on him? I was doing him no favours by letting him stay in my apartment. A few days later I told him it was time to move on. He was shocked.

'You mean you want me to leave?'

'Yes.'

'Where will I go?'

'I don't know.'

As he was packing I asked him, 'Do you feel loved?'

'Yes.'

'By me?'

'Yes.'

'Do you feel loved by your father?'

'Yes.'

But he was angry and he didn't return my texts. And I shed silent tears each night for about a year. Sometimes Nick heard me and he would put his arms around me and hold me tight.

I remembered a story that moved me very much. When George was about seven, he and his father and I went to a party in the country. The host, a farmer, told me that when his son turned eighteen he had asked him to come into the living room for a talk. He told his son that he would never again tell him what to do. Then he stood up and went into his bedroom and wept for hours. I never forgot the image I had formed in my mind of that big strong farmer with enormous tanned forearms, sobbing on his bed.

What about my resentment? Would I be able to let it go?

Nick wanted to please his children. He used to change out of his good clothes into his old ones before he saw his children: he would take off his two-year-old chinos and put on his four-year-old pair, take off his smart grey shirt and put on a faded blue one, frayed at the collar and around the cuffs. If he was seeing Antony he wouldn't wear his new leather jacket with the zip, the one I had bought for him at Daffy's Bargain Basement on Broadway for a hundred and twenty dollars; he would wear his old one. Nick was wearing his new leather jacket from Daffy's when he was killed. I thought about that a lot.

•

In 2010 I went to the Notre Dame to pray for Nick's mother. I lit a candle for her. In a few days I would take the train from Paris to London to visit her. I wanted to see her because Nick would want me to. Also, I wanted to know what she would ask me about her son. I wanted to give her something. I thought I would take her flowers. Not pink ones or red or orange. White. The colour of unity. And not too many.

'I'll show her that I can forgive her,' I told Catherine de Clippel, a friend in Paris.

'She wants to see you?' she said.

'She said she would. I won't be rude to her.'

'Of course you won't.'

'I'd like to be,' I said shamefully.

Catherine suggested I take cookies. 'They're easier than flowers. That way she won't have to go through the cupboards looking for a vase. She can just put them on the table.'

I love flowers. I am profoundly moved by them. When Nick and I were courting I sent him a dozen yellow roses from New York. Felicity, a co-curator, was in Nick's office when they arrived and said, 'Are you being courted?' Apparently, Nick blushed.

Camilla and I bought a dozen red garden roses for the homicide detective after he found Antony.

When I'd gone to the florist to choose some flowers for Steve, the girl suggested hothouse roses. I looked at them. 'They're for a priest,' I said.

'Not roses,' she said, and showed me tulips.

I saw a tiny bunch of white bellflowers. 'I'll take those,' I said. They were from a field and they had a strong scent. 'Wildflowers with a scent, just right for a Jesuit priest,' I thought.

I spent at least an hour in the food hall at Bon Marché in Paris, trying to decide which biscuits to buy. I wanted a pretty package with a French design and for the cookies to be plain, not too fancy or rich or hard. I finally chose some old-fashioned country-style galettes in a cream box with royal-blue writing. I'd give her the piece on Nick I wrote for the magazine *Art and Australia*. And I'd tell her how much I loved her son. Then I'd leave.

•

I walked to the Luxembourg Gardens and adored the chestnuts in bloom. I walked past the palm trees and olives that had been wheeled out of their winter glasshouse, like giraffes, let out for some sun and fresh air. And I went along the track where Nick and I used to collapse with laughter watching the French runners, with their delightfully uncoordinated ape-like upper bodies and duck-footed shuffles. I stopped at the Medici Fountain: I had always thought the bronze sculpture was Bacchus leaning over the rocky outcrop and secretly admiring the two lovers below. But the night before I had looked it up on the internet and discovered that the fountain depicts the jealous one-eyed giant Polyphemus, who has surprised Acis and Galatea and will shortly kill Acis. Then Galatea, in her grief, will turn the blood of Acis into a river. (My misinterpretation of this story had much to do with Nick's.) What we think is love is actually envy.

After the funeral, I kept hearing the same words from many different people: 'Nick loved me.' A woman who worked with him confided in me: 'I will never be loved by anyone as much as Nick loved me.' I felt a slight twinge of jealousy but only for twenty seconds because I knew she meant it. I knew Nick could love that many people. It was his quality of attention and genuine interest.

'When he greeted me he was always so interested—and surprised,' said artist Imants Tillers.

'He was like that with everyone,' I said.

'Oh really, I thought he was just like that with me,' he said jokingly.

'He liked me, he really did. We had something. I felt it when I first met him. He made me feel important,' said a woman.

'He made everyone feel that way,' I said.

'Really?'

Nick was a lover. He loved everyone. He made me feel special, too, but I knew it wasn't just me. He made everyone feel special. And he meant it. You can't pull that off for years with so many people and not mean it. On the train to London, I sat next to a politician and she told me she had met Barack Obama. 'In that one micro-second meeting with him,' she said, 'he made me feel I was the most important person in the world.'

Visiting Nick's mother

Nick's old friends John and Zoe had emailed me: Nick's mother was amenable to seeing me. They offered to take me, adding that it was a meeting they didn't relish, but as they had known Baba and Nick for so long they would do what they could. They picked me up at the Chelsea Arts Club, which had graciously transferred Nick's membership to me, and drove me to Nick's mother's house. They had bought champagne and orange juice.

A cousin of Nick's, Kate, let us in. We entered and Nick's mother was standing in the middle of the sitting room, a gaunt figure, bent over. She was facing away and gave me a sideways glance, her head cocked to one side, which made her large wig look as if it had slipped. I hesitated for a moment, then crossed the room and gave her a kiss. I gave her the packet of chocolate galettes; she looked at them disapprovingly and said, 'Oh,' and put them on the table. On the bookshelves were scattered an incredible number of photographs, many more than I remembered from previous visits. She must have been riffling through her old photo albums. There were photographs of Nick and his children and his first partner. There were many of Antony as a baby and as a child.

John and Zoe opened the champagne and talked about the traffic. I looked at Baba and asked, 'How are you feeling?'

'I really do feel as if I am ninety-two now,' she said with a sigh. 'I've never felt ninety-two before.' She sat down in her chair in the corner. 'I've been in touch with Antony.' She glanced at Zoe. 'I don't suppose you approve.'

'I don't,' said Zoe.

'Antony has been having a terrible time of it in jail,' she said with an evasive eye. 'Apparently, somehow or other, the prisoners got wind of the fact that Antony had "touched" a child and they have been giving him a terrible time.'

'Antony didn't "touch" the child,' I said. 'He sliced her throat with a knife.'

Baba continued as if I had remarked on the weather, 'He has sold some of his paintings.'

I wanted to ask why he would need to do that now but stopped myself. She looked at me directly. 'He doesn't remember what he did, you know.'

I reminded her that Antony went into hiding for ten days and that the whole country was out looking for him. 'People were terrified. My friends went to the parks with baseball bats looking for him.'

Nick's mother didn't respond. She pointed to a photograph of Nick and told me she had been sent a copy of *Art and Australia*. 'There are articles in honour of him.

I had no idea he was so well respected and loved,' she said. 'Why on earth didn't he tell me?'

'Why didn't he tell you?' I stammered. 'But you knew he worked hard.' Nick used to ring his mother every Sunday evening and I would overhear him telling her all that he had done during the week.

'Oh, did he work hard?'

'Yes, he worked hard each day and night until very late, and always for others.'

'Oh? I think he should have told me. He could have said it jokingly somehow. Just to let me know.'

I downed my glass of too-sweet champagne, which tasted bitter, and thought if only I could have taken Nick to an island. But we had been living in Australia, on an island and far from this place. I needed to get him away, to another island.

Zoe refilled my glass. I wished it were whisky straight up. I looked at the yellowing walls and thought they had been papered with resentment. Every stitch on the needlepoint cushions had been threaded with resentment.

Baba asked if I had met Ben.

'Only briefly.'

'Oh, really?' she said, feigning ignorance with great skill. 'Why is that?'

'Well, because he and Chloe wouldn't allow me into their house or to any family gatherings. Didn't you know?'

'Really? Why would anyone do that?'

Now I had to say it. 'Well, you did that.'

'Did I?'

'Yes.'

'How?' She looked baffled.

'You didn't let me attend your son's memorial.'

'Oh, that!' She raised her hand and put it on her breast. 'That was something between me and myself.'

'Me and myself . . .'

Baba switched the subject to her great-grandchildren. 'I speak to the girl, she's just like Chloe. She says, "Hello, Baba" and all these things I can't make out. The little boy sits in the background and just says faintly, "Hello."'

John saw my empty glass and poured me another drink. I was the only one drinking.

Baba said, 'Ben told me that when they went back to the house, as they were entering the front door the little boy asked him, "Will I see red?"' Her manner was so fey it was as if she was describing a sunset.

'What has this child seen?' I thought. We were discussing horror and passing chips to one another.

Baba told me that Chloe was always complaining that her parents-in-law didn't do enough to help her with the kids. 'Well, they are now, apparently,' she said, seeming enlivened by her dialogue, her eyes glittering. I was burning up. My face must have been red.

She glanced at me sideways. 'I'm on two sticks now and I can't move two of my fingers.'

I remembered Jane's words when she came to a party at our place ten years ago: 'Nick is walking around in a bubble of love.' I was sceptical. 'Oh yeah?' But now I do think Nick lived in a bubble of love, and he had created it, just like the bubble in Bosch's *Garden of Earthly Delights*, the glass sphere in which the couple are caressing and illustrating the Dutch proverb 'Happiness and glass. How soon shall they pass.'

John stood up and made an excuse. 'We have to get you to your dinner, Juliet.'

We rose. I thanked Baba for having me. She gave me a photograph of Nick.

'Come back again and visit me,' she said with a knowing look.

It was impossible for me to smile. Did this woman think she was going to live forever? She hadn't asked a single question about her son, his funeral or his remains.

It was a relief to walk out into the cold spring air.

I went back to my room at the Chelsea Arts Club and looked at the photograph of Nick sitting sideways on a chair wearing a costume, a purple and gold Chinese robe, and holding a splayed fan, posing for the camera. It didn't hurt anymore to look at his kind, gentle face.

•

The next day from the phone booth in the foyer I rang Ginny, who used to be my nanny, and who looked after my sister and me for a while when we were kids. She now lived in Canterbury. 'Hello, Ginny. It's Juliet.'

Without hesitation, she asked, 'What has happened? You sound so sad.'

I didn't expect her question and burst into tears. A woman I had only seen once since I was a child had heard me.

'I am. I am.' I told her what had happened to Nick.

All day I lay on the bed crying. I couldn't stop. A few times someone knocked on the door to check the plumbing in the basin. There was nothing wrong with the sink. Perhaps they were checking on me because they could hear me weeping.

I went to John Sandoe's bookshop, climbed down the steep stairs and found the poetry section. I stood before the books and wept. As I walked down the Kings Road, hot tears were pouring down my face. On a bench in Duke of York Square I wept. No one looked at me.

Nick's ashes

It was one year since Nick had died. I was kneeling in the blue shadows under the jacaranda, where the flowers had fallen, putting petals into a basket when a woman with a young girl in school uniform stopped to watch me. The mother asked, 'What are those for?'

'They're for my partner. He died. We're laying his ashes.'

'How did he die?'

I looked at her eight-year-old daughter, and wondered if I should say it in front of her. Then I heard it: 'He was murdered.'

I had said it, in the street, for her and for myself. I said it to try to make it real. Because I still don't believe it.

'Not Nick Waterlow,' she said.

'Yes.'

'I knew him.'

Another woman was walking past us and without stopping she called back, smiling, 'Oh, I knew him too. I knew Nick Waterlow.'

•

I went to St Canice's and sat on the floor in front of the niches and bowed my head. It was dark and quiet and cool, and the light shone on the icon, which was burnt at one corner. I lit a tea candle in front of the niches and prayed. When I stepped out of the church an Aboriginal woman who was sitting on her mattress under the alcove and brushing her hair said something I didn't hear.

'What?'

'Who's in there?' she said.

'No one. Just me.'

'What were you doing in there?'

'Saying a prayer. I was praying.'

When I heard myself answer her, it felt good to tell someone what I had been doing in there.

•

I was going to play a piece at the ceremony to lay Nick's ashes and I wanted to hear how it would sound on the church piano. As I unlocked the cover of the piano I noticed a man in a white jacket wearing a backpack leaning on the altar in front of the Statue of the Sacred Heart. I began to play and the man drifted across the nave; he moved from one pew to another, each time getting closer. Eventually he came to the pew next to the piano, and sat listening, like a blind man behind his sunglasses. I played clumsily but the delicate minor notes and Freygish scales in the upper register sounded beautiful in the empty church.

When I had finished, the man crossed himself. 'You're an angel,' he said.

I had seen him sleeping on the porch of the church, and as he rose I asked, 'Are you a friend of Steve's?'

He turned sideways, looked away and muttered, 'Yes.' He made a move towards the door then suddenly retraced his steps, coming up close. He fixed his sad eyes upon me. 'He's my best friend.'

•

The following day I arranged to meet my friend Andrew Kotatko, a film-maker. I found him sitting in a pew listening to Joseph, who was playing Beethoven. I had seen this man before, hovering over some flower arrangements left over from a funeral. He had looked up, seen me and said, 'I *love* flowers.'

Andrew said, 'He came over and asked me if I'd like to hear him play a little Chopin and I said, "Yes please." Then, for some reason, he sat down and played Beethoven.'

I came across Joseph again one afternoon when I was arranging some waterlilies on the altar. He asked me my name and when I told him he stood and kissed my hand with a flourish. Then he squealed, and his whole body quivered. I laughed. He asked me what the waterlilies were for. I told him that they were a symbol of eternal life and compassion for my partner.

'Do you communicate with him?' he said.

'No,' I said. 'But I feel, somehow, I'm in that other world, in the shadows, connected with the dead, all the dead, from all times.'

'Spooky,' he said.

•

My eyes stung when I found a note in Nick's handwriting among his papers. *I wish my father hadn't been cremated. Then there would have been a place for me to be close to him.*

I wondered if I should have buried Nick instead of cremating him. Before the funeral I'd asked Steve if there was a plot kept for Nick next to his first partner. He said, 'No. He had moved on. Also, we don't bury people anymore.'

•

I had been given two tickets to see Leonard Cohen at the Sydney Stadium. I had invited Steve to join me. It was the night before the laying of Nick's ashes. I arrived at St Canice's and found Steve in the church holding a screwdriver; he was replacing a damaged plaque on one of the niches. Steve told me Nick's ashes hadn't arrived. We went to his office and he looked through the telephone book to find the funeral home's number. I panicked and thought maybe they really had lost them. From Paris, I had sent the funeral home a flurry of emails asking if they could keep his ashes for another six months. When I didn't hear back from them immediately I thought that perhaps they had gone astray. They eventually sent me an email assuring me that 'he was safe' and they would keep 'him' until I was ready. Him? They referred to his ashes as they would a living person. Nick was now a pile of ashes.

Steve calmly made a call to the funeral home and then told me that they would deliver them the next morning. Then he turned to me and said very seriously, 'I don't mean to be glib, but the greatest gift Nick has given you is his death.' How could that be? I wanted Nick, not his death. Everything hurt: every sight, sound and surface. Later when I told a friend, she said, 'Did he explain?' 'No.' I mentioned it to Andrew who said, 'He must have given that a lot of thought. That's not something you say without thinking about it.'

Steve had just celebrated a funeral mass and he was wearing a black shirt. He changed into a Hawaiian shirt and we took the train to the concert.

As we made our way out of the auditorium after the concert and joined the throng heading for the door, Steve said, 'Passion. That's what it's all about. That's what religion is all about. People forget that. They get caught up with their minds.'

I rolled a cigarette and I needed to bum a light. A middle-aged woman was walking towards me. She came right up to me, out of the dark, her face streaked with mascara. 'I'm going to play the CD in the morning,' she said. She gave me a light and as she walked off alone into the dark she called out again, 'I'm going to play the CD in the morning.'

•

I arrived at St Canice's to meet Eddie Bronson at eleven. My mother was there also, looking sheepish. I asked her why she was there so early because I had already rung her especially to tell her the ceremony began at noon. She said hesitantly, 'Yes, I know ... but I wanted to make sure.' I thought with irritation, 'She's reminding me that she has never trusted me.' But also I saw that I could accept that too. If she couldn't trust me, that was no longer my problem. Through my mother, I could see myself as a child and also again as a mother with my son. And I saw her as a child. It was so clear to me that my mother's inability to trust was something I was never going to be able to change. And I thought, 'It is good to be reminded how important it is to trust one's child.' When I told Andrew he laughed. 'Why wouldn't your own mother trust you?'

•

I had called Eddie and asked him if he would play.

'I can do that. What do you want me to play? The same thing I played at the funeral?'

'No. Something different, something happier, something with . . . gratitude.'

'You want something happy. You should have the accordion.'

'No. The accordion is sad. Just the sax, please.'

'But a solo instrument is very sad. Better you have two instruments.'

'No, no. Really, I just want you, just you, playing the sax. Just a single instrument.'

'But a solo instrument is always sad. It will be very sad.'

'Then, Eddie, I want it to be sad. Maybe you can play a duet with me. Although I might be scared to play on my own.'

'Oy! I'm scared to play with you!'

'We'll practise. I'll play the piano and you can play the clarinet. We'll do it for Nick. Come on, he would love it. We'll try.'

My friend Gemma taught me the piece and told me I had to play it fifty times a day, so I kept a log, and ticked it off each time I played it. I wondered if my neighbours were doing the same. I could only manage to play it thirty times before I was sick of it. For all my practice the piece never sounded any better.

I was practising when Eddie walked in the door. 'Sounds good,' he said. He looked at the piano, impressed. 'How come there's a grand piano in a church? It's a big thing to have a piano in a place like this. It's not just for looking at. I've never seen it. I will tell all my jazz friends about it.'

Friends Paul and Sally arranged branches of flowering jacaranda in battered rusty drums, wabi-sabi-style, near the piano and on the candle stand in front of the niches. On the side altar we placed two large bunches of white waterlilies.

•

The church filled up with people and I felt my hands stiffening and I asked Eddie, 'Do you think I can do this? Can I play this?'

'Oy, if you let your emotions take over your mind you won't be able to play. If you let your mind take over your emotions you will be able to play. Good luck! There is nowhere to hide.' His face was like stone.

I saw Steve walk through the church holding the container with Nick's ashes. I followed him into the sacristy. He asked me, 'How did you sleep?'

'Not very well. Hardly at all.'

He opened the plastic container with a screwdriver and held the container out to me. 'It is good to look.'

I looked through the circular opening and saw the white chalky granules—Nick's bones, his skull, his hands. I heard the homicide detective's words: 'It all happened pretty quickly.'

Walking back out into the church I saw Stas, George's childhood friend. He gave me a big hug. I told him, 'I love you,' and he said, 'I love you too.'

I could feel a pain as sharp as light as I read the Rumi poem, the first line of which was engraved into Nick's niche:

In your light I learn how to love
In your beauty, how to make poems.
You dance inside my chest
Where no one sees you,
But sometimes I do,
And that sight becomes this art.

Luke read from the Book of Job.

Steve was dressed in his trademark Hawaiian shirt and wore a colourful stole around his neck; he told us that it had been made for him by a mother who had lost her son. As he spoke a wave of grief began to rise in my chest and take hold of my throat.

Steve turned to me and gestured for me to begin. I walked to the piano and, fighting back the desire to sob aloud, I sat down and began to play. After a while I looked up and saw Eddie standing in front of me, ready with his clarinet. He nodded and together we played 'A Brivele Der Mamen' by Denis Cuniot, then 'Peace Piece' by Bill Evans. I don't know how I played because I wasn't inside the sound and I wasn't inside the church. I was somewhere far away. Then Eddie picked up his sax and began his solo improvisation 'Psalm'. A series of long grave notes cast heavy clouds over the atmosphere. They went down and down into the darkness. He was conjuring Nick's spirit, he caught it and then played with it, he loved it and he cried to it and held it up for us all, and then, still playing, he walked out of the church and into the street. I stood and with a will not my own I followed him out to the steps. He played his last note to the sky and suddenly dropped his head as if he had been hit from behind.

'Oh, Eddie, that was beautiful, just beautiful. Maybe when people are leaving you could play some more?'

He looked exhausted. 'No,' he said firmly. 'I have done it.'

'Yes, you have,' I said.

He stood unmoving, like a statue, and I kissed him on the cheek.

•

A tiny diamond had fallen out of the eternity ring Nick had given me. I wanted to replace it, not with a diamond but with a ruby, to remind myself that nothing would ever be the same again, and if I wished that things were different, or if I ever forgot the pain, I would only have to look at my ring. Also, it would represent the imperfect, the impermanent, the incomplete. With his jewellery glasses on and a pair of tweezers, Robb Gardner spent much time going through his box of rubies, trying to find one small enough; he needed one the size of a piece of cracked pepper. He found one and dropped it and, while he was looking for it under his papers, I told him I had cracked all my back teeth and lost all the fillings. He looked up at me over his glasses and said, 'It often happens when there is a loss. Such things happen. A stone often falls out of a ring.'

PART FOUR

A double spring

So you think you're still alive, then?

Gaius Caesar

I am in Paris in spring. Nick and I were to have been here together at the Cité Internationale des Arts. I have flown across the earth to experience the same season—a double spring. Double the bitterness, double the beauty.

'Don't go to Paris alone,' said Steve. 'You'll be lonely in Paris on your own.'

'I won't be,' I told him. 'There's no room for it.'

I wasn't lonely, even though I passed the couples holding hands and leaning on the Pont Neuf, gazing at the shimmering bands of gold and silver light on the water. No, it didn't make me feel lonely to look at them—no lonelier than it did to look at the dusty pink flowers of the chestnuts behind Notre Dame.

I wandered through the streets with my eyes to the ground, searching the thousand-year-old cobblestones for answers. They didn't reply. The muscles under my chin were so strained and prominent from weeping that it affected the way I walked. I told myself, 'I can believe it. But I can't believe it, and yet . . .' On my way to the Metro a pregnant woman saw me muttering audibly to myself and smiled faintly. What did she see?

Pain had sealed my mouth. I could feel the pain in the ends of my hair. My face was so tense it hurt to touch it. If I looked at myself in the mirror, it wasn't because I wanted to see my reflection; it was that I wanted Nick to see me.

I filled the kettle. I couldn't believe it. I fried an egg, and I looked at it, and I couldn't believe it.

A group of residents attending a French class at the Cité Internationale des Arts walked down the Champs-Élysées at three in the morning. It was 1 May, International Workers' Day. There were still many cars on the road, with drivers leaning out their windows, honking their horns, and as they passed, their car lights turned the pale flowers of the chestnut trees into lanterns. We had been to a dinner at our French teacher's house. Victor, a Lithuanian, one of the very talented pianists at the Cité, played Chopin's 'Ballade No. 1' on a little broken upright piano until a neighbour complained.

Earlier that afternoon I heard the Ballade drifting into the street from Victor's window. I told Victor later that I had stopped under his window to listen to him.

'When I practise,' he said drily, 'always there are one or two people in the street. They clap.'

I told him I had been trying to find a piano, but the administrators of the art school wouldn't let me have one because I had told the secretary I hadn't passed the music exams.

'Some people who are not professional can play better than professionals. There are pianists who have given their whole lives to the piano and they play like dogs,' said Victor.

•

I wandered through the streets to admire the faint new growth on the old trees and the pink balls of cherry blossom in the cold white air. Outside my window the brown stems of ivy on the four-hundred-year-old stone wall were just tinged with green. The leaves would grow and soon the grey limestone wall would be covered. I remembered my friend Mimi Haskell, not long before she died, looking out at the oak trees in the snow and telling me: 'They look beautiful without their leaves only because we know they are going to come back to life.'

As a child my mother was so frightened of death. At the mention of the word she would run out of the room weeping. My father caught me reading a book called *The Hour of Our Death*, and he told me that he found it odd that I was so interested in death when I was still so young. He'd been through the war as a fighter pilot and he said that ever since he'd never given it a second thought. I wondered why he didn't think about it. Perhaps my mother's fear of death was the reason for my fascination. I was afraid of her fear. I think I wanted to discover why she was so frightened.

When we were fly-fishing in a remote mountain valley, my ten-year-old son George had an encounter with a yellow-bellied black snake. He trod on it and the snake rose up and followed him, its head flattened out ready to strike, but then George turned around, and he and the snake, at the same height, faced one another for what seemed to be an endless amount of time. Then, as suddenly as it rose up, the snake dropped to the ground and slid away. As we took the long walk back to the car I noticed one snake and then another curled up on every sunny rock, and at each sighting I screamed. For at least a year after that George wanted me to take him to the library to show him pictures and read books to him about every kind of snake.

•

When Nick and I first went to Paris we lit candles in Notre Dame. I remember asking him if the candles were for the dead. 'They're not just for the dead,' he said. I lit my candle for George and I prayed: 'Lord protect my child.' I wonder now if Nick lit a candle for Antony. I never considered that one day I would be lighting candles for Nick.

From my studio, I could hear the bells from Notre Dame, Saint-Gervais and Saint-Paul-Saint-Louis. I prayed for Nick whenever I heard them. I used to think that prayer was a way to give thanks. Now I know that prayer is also a creative act, an act bringing into this world something new, a wishing that allows us to connect ourselves to our souls, and to others, to the living and to the dead.

•

I accepted the kind hospitality of a nagging wife who berated her husband for using the wrong plate to serve the takeaway sushi which he had picked up. While we were eating he made sure to tell me that his wife was the one who paid for it. I listened to a couple skyping one another to talk about their haircuts and mobile phone bills. An academic and his wife held hands at the table and talked about the efficiency of lycra clothing for travel. A husband left the lunch table mid-meal to get to a rendezvous with his mistress. All these incidents made me want to stand up and head for the bathroom in order to weep.

The bells of Saint-Gervais were ringing. I prayed that I would not lose my belief in the sincerity of human beings and that they were not all secretly indifferent to one another. Next door an elderly couple were talking animatedly. I didn't understand what they were saying but I prayed that they were 'relating'.

•

I was trying to enjoy my Montaigne essays, alone in a very romantic restaurant at a candlelit table set for two. My steak, on top of which a large bunch of dried thyme was on fire and smoking, was carried by a waitress with a kind face and one arm in plaster across the room and placed on the table in front of me. At a nearby table, an elderly couple were laughing loudly, convulsively; every now and then they would erupt in sync. It was beautiful to listen to their laughter. It was how Nick and I laughed. It was how Nick and I spent almost every meal together, laughing. Laughter was our language. In bed, too, although in that sacred place our laughter was a serious matter.

•

I went to the lingerie department change rooms at Bon Marché. An elderly woman was changing in the next booth. Her husband, also in his eighties, was sitting on a sofa holding on to his walking stick, waiting for her to open the curtain and show herself to him. As a young girl, I didn't watch the young couples, I studied the elderly couples walking hand in hand; I was in awe of them, and I used to wish that one day, when I was an old woman, I would have such a relationship with an old man.

•

In Tuscany, Jane Campion and I walked from Bagno Vignoni to Pienza. After five hours wandering through a Leonardo da Vinci landscape, sighting the town and then losing it again, we entered the outskirts of Pienza and came upon a charming little stone church. Rice and tiny white paper hearts were scattered over the gravel outside the doorway. Jane picked up a few paper hearts and gave them to me. I stuffed them in my pocket. We sat for a while in a pew in the cool empty church. The wedding must have been that day because the flowers were still fresh in their vases. If there was ever a church in which to be married, this was it. 'This is where I want to marry Nick,' I thought.

Strange familiar

In our apartment in Sydney everything was still where it was when I left. I picked up Nick's black rubber sneakers, which had collapsed after leaning on the banister for ten months, and I kissed them. I walked out of the building and saw Attila, the gardener. He smiled. I looked straight at him. 'Do you know what happened to Nick? Did you hear?' I burst into tears. He came up and gave me a hug and held me tight. It felt good to be hugged by this stranger, a man I barely knew. Then he let go of me and looked up at the sky. 'We've had good spring rain. Spring is here.' He pointed to the white rosebush in the tub. 'The roses will soon be in bloom. And did you notice the jacaranda for Nick over there on the median strip? I planted it. It's doing well.'

The tree is blooming years before it should; its tender branches are bobbing with the weight of birds.

'He's not about here, you know,' said Attila. 'If that's what you're thinking. He's not walking the place. I can tell you that for sure.'

I wander through the rooms of our apartment trying to recognise what I see. When I empty the fridge I notice the expiry date on the jar of English mustard and recall Nick reading the label and laughing and asking me, 'Where do you think English mustard is made?'

'I don't know.'

'Take a guess.'

'France?' I say.

'In China!'

I see Nick's expiry date in an ink stamp: 9/11/2009. It is stamped on my soul.

•

I turn to leave the kitchen and I am summoned by a blue cloud, which fills the bedroom window frame. It is a jacaranda. Outside, clusters of blue petals float in the air like mist. In my car, I swing around a corner, and blue trees suddenly appear; one sways about a low red roof, another reaches over the roadway; a nervous flash of blue passes through my rear-view mirror. The bell-shaped petals are already falling and they lie along the gutters and over parked cars, caught in windscreen wiper blades. I shake my head at the unreality of those ephemeral flowers. I look at them, at the strangeness of them, for they need to be imagined, and this spring, after all the rain they are bolder, more insistent than ever. They speak to me in their language without words, repeating their message, over and over—with colour, with blue. 'Don't forget,' they whisper, 'when the world turns black, when something ends, something new begins.' I don't want to hear. I'm not ready to begin. They don't care what I think. I turn my head away but they are there, behind me. They refuse to be ignored—and they refuse to be sorrowed over.

•

When I was helping Nick to clean up under his beach house, I found two shotguns. I insisted he remove them, and so he brought them in their case to our apartment and put them under our bed. One morning, while feeling around for my shoe, I found them and put them in the high cupboard. I forgot about them for a while. Finally, two weeks before he died, I said, 'Nick, like it or not, I'm getting rid of those guns. I'm not living with them any longer. And you're not giving them to anyone.'

I wrapped them in a beach towel; outside the pub in Queen Street, Woollahra, I gave them to a friend who put them in the boot of his car. He would arrange to have them sold.

After Nick's death, Luke asked me for the guns.

'What for?' I said.

Luke said he had a sentimental attachment to them because they had belonged to his grandfather and his initials were on the case.

I told him, 'No way. You're never getting those guns. You can't have a firearm without a licence.'

Luke was silent for a moment and then said, 'I want to bury them with my father's ashes at my mother's grave.'

'If I ever wrote this no one would believe me,' I thought. I could imagine why he might want to bury the guns.

'Well, that's not going to happen either,' I said to Luke.

•

Grief does strange things. Luke and I were in the lawyer's office signing a statutory declaration when his mobile rang. He held it out to me. 'Do you want to answer it?'

I said, 'No, I don't want to answer it. It's your call. It's your telephone.'

I was reminded of the time just before Nick's memorial when Luke asked me what I wanted him to say about me. I'm sure he meant well but I told him, probably too curtly, 'Don't ask me to tell you what to say. Say whatever you want. Please.'

•

It was Sunday evening when I met Luke again. All the places to eat were closed except for the pub that I had refused on principle to enter because they had pokies. However, that evening I didn't have the energy to go further afield and I agreed to enter the place I had managed for the last few years to avoid. But if 'all the world's a stage'—and Shakespeare was definitely an artist for the future—then it was probably an appropriate place to meet.

Antony had been given large amounts of cash over the years, and in the two years leading up to the deaths he went through over half a million dollars, buying works of art which he would put into his storage unit and spending the rest on alcohol and pokies. He had only a few cents in his account on the day he committed the murders.

Nick had signed a binding agreement with his children that half the proceeds of all assets would be divided equally among them. I had found among Nick's papers his attempts with lawyers to put Antony's money into trust but this was not possible unless all parties agreed. Luke and Chloe wanted Antony to have his money in cash, and so did Antony.

We entered a dimly lit room with throbbing 'let's get it on' music and Luke ordered a drink from a brittle waitress. He talked about his family and told me that his mother had a special relationship with Antony. Then he skipped a few years and said his parents were never around. Then he said they had dinner together every night. He had tried to talk to his mother but he couldn't because she wasn't 'available'; however, he also said that she wanted to please. 'It was a perfect childhood, with holidays and birthday parties and new shoes,' he said. 'But it wasn't perfect.' The more he talked the less I understood.

A few days later I showed Luke his father's car. I opened the boot, which was still full of papers and art catalogues. Luke saw a grey baseball cap, and he picked it up, pressed it hard into his face, and inhaled. All at once, as if suddenly remembering something, he took it from his face and asked apprehensively, 'Is this Dad's?'

'Yes,' I said.

Luke shuddered. 'I hope to God it's not my brother's!' Then he laughed.

I looked at Luke's face and heard those saddest of words over again: 'not my brother's'.

I told Luke that Camilla and I had found Antony's backpack in the boot of the car. We went through it and found a list of videos he had borrowed from Marrickville library. One of the titles was *Family Plot* by Hitchcock. I'd told the police and asked them if they thought it was of any significance. 'No, just normal viewing fare,' the homicide detective had said.

'So Dad drove Antony to Chloe's?' Luke asked.

'That's what the police think,' I said.

Luke told me that when he viewed Chloe and Nick at the morgue, Chloe looked as if she had fought for her life, every vein was strained and showing on her arms, but Nick looked relatively peaceful. Perhaps Nick hadn't fought? But there were numerous defence wounds on his arms and hands; he *had* fought for his life.

Luke asked me if I thought his father had been happy before he died. 'I don't mean with you,' he said.

I told him 'yes'. But as soon as the words left my mouth I knew I had told a lie. I corrected myself: 'Yes, Nick was happy, and no, he wasn't.'

On our morning walks, Nick and I always passed a pretty pink house and we used to speculate on why the blinds and curtains were permanently closed. We imagined the white liquid we noticed trickling from the house drain into the gutter in the street was a waste product from a secret criminal activity. One day the house was cordoned off with tape and we read in the papers that the husband had murdered his wife. After that, we always walked on the other side of the street.

We think these stories are for others but they belong to us all. I haven't seen a film since Nick died. For me films are no longer real enough.

I remember when David Malouf and I were sitting in Roslyn and Tony Oxley's house and I noticed two guests walking out the front door. I said to David, 'Whenever I see someone departing I think of death. We're all on our way to the grave.' It was before Nick died.

I thought I knew it then, but I was just saying it. I used to think our days would go on forever.

About two months after Nick died, David invited me to the opening night of *Hamlet* at the Sydney Theatre Company. I watched the opening scene, in which the actors struggled comically with the coffin, trying to place it into the grave, and I wondered if I would be able to watch the whole play. I had my hand over my mouth for the entire performance. I was familiar with the play, as we used to perform it as children in the courtyard at my grandmother's farm. We have all heard those famous words so many times and I had thought of them as a conceit, but that night the words 'All the world's a stage' took on a new significance and I was immeasurably comforted to know that someone else had lived on this earth who had truly understood the state of grief and was able to express it.

As we left the theatre David said, 'Today Hamlet would be considered bipolar.'

I didn't think he was bipolar. 'No. I don't think so. Hamlet was sane. He was just grieving.'

•

Nick's body was found near the front door. 'He nearly got away,' said a friend. Another said, 'You know, maybe it was just bad luck.'

'No. It had to happen,' I thought, and recalled the words of Montaigne: 'Everyone finds their own death. Especially in the natures of men, there are hidden parts which cannot be divined, silent characteristics which are never revealed and which are sometimes unknown even to the one who has them but which are awakened and brought out by subsequent events.'

If these parts of his nature were unknown to Nick, it wasn't for lack of thought on his part. I never knew a man who gave so much thought to every big and little thing.

One day one of us will be lost to the other

I am between two worlds, between two waves.

It hurts to hear the sound of the Australian birds. Is it because they remind me of what Nick can no longer hear, or is it that the cry is from a place so far away, and yet it still reaches into my heart? It crosses space and time, and takes me with it. I am back in the apartment where the terracotta path, the blue front door, the datura, the marble kitchen table are familiar but not quite recognisable anymore: they are all so much further away than before. But something else has changed. I can hear the police sirens. They used to make me hold my breath but now they don't bother me at all.

•

My agent had asked, 'Do you talk to Nick?'

'No. He's dead,' I said.

I picked a magnolia grandiflora and placed it in a green vase on the kitchen table. As I was having my dinner I was admiring the ancient blossom against its glossy dark green leaves and I began to talk, and when I awoke from my stupor I realised I had been talking to the flower, and I had been talking to Nick.

Two birds had flown in through the window. As I came into the kitchen I saw them walking about on the black linoleum floor. I shook my apron and with a broom tried to head them towards the open window. They flew away so quickly I didn't see them: I just felt their wings.

Then I saw their droppings on the day bed, and that my open book on the kitchen table was splattered with gold: Jackson Pollock might have done it. Gold shit was splashed across the page of an illustration of a standing Buddha 'Calling for Rain', a wooden figure of a woman in gold lacquer with a serene smile on her face, her arms by her side, her fingers to the ground. In a museum in Bordeaux I stopped at the Van Goyen landscape of a tree struck by lightning, an unusual subject, and I remembered the jacaranda tree in the COFA courtyard, which had been violently struck in the same way on the night of Nick's death.

At a retreat in the south of France, I was in the garden talking about Nick to a group when a pair of butterflies flew into the centre of our circle and hovered, fluttering a few feet above the ground. The young nun stopped me and said, 'Look.'

For months there has been the same grasshopper in the shower behind the soap or on the bedroom wall. I do believe, and I scarcely dare say it, but I know there is a spirit.

•

I was sitting in my parked car listening to Glenn Gould's the *Goldberg Variations*—the notes, formal like pain, erotic, and achingly vulnerable. Nick's only outstanding debt had been his drycleaning. As I'd entered the drycleaners I recognised Nick's shirts and trousers in plastic shrouds; they had been pulled out and were hanging in a group on their own. The drycleaner seemed surprised when I asked for them, and he handed them to me without saying a word. I didn't say anything to him either. I paid for them and left. So he had heard the news too. Probably he had watched it on his television on the wall. It was always on. Nick and I started taking our laundry to him when he first opened his business, and for two years he never said a word to us. We laughed about this, and then later we laughed about the fact that one day, for no particular reason, he began to talk; and he didn't just talk, he gave us his opinions on the global warming, on sport, on politics. Now he was silent again. I'd taken Nick's clothes home and hung them in the cupboard. Now his old clothes were in the back seat of my car on their way to the charity bin at the church. That morning I had picked up his Japanese dressing gown with a pattern of exploding firecrackers; his smell was on it. I wasn't ready to part with that, not yet. He had such a beautiful smell: musty and earthy, salty, not at all sour. The art curator Johnnie Walker walked through the front door of the apartment he immediately said, 'I can smell Nick. He had a beautiful smell.' Marta said, 'It never goes away, you know.'

My mobile rang and I turned down the Bach and answered it. It was Ross. 'I have a book of erotic art that belongs to Nick. Somehow it came into my possession. I'm not quite sure why Nick gave it to me. I think he was asking me to hold it for him. I'm not really certain. It wasn't a gift, I know that. Anyhow, I kept it wrapped in paper on one of the bottom shelves.' Ross suggested we meet so he could return it to me.

'I'm keen to look at it,' I said.

Dreaming of reality

The day after Nick died, Jane Campion dreamt that she saw him as an angel with huge jacaranda-blue wings and he was wearing yellow trousers. The artist Tim Johnson told me that on the evening before Nick died he was walking home from his studio and he saw a cross made from clouds moving slowly across the sky, lit by the moon. He told his studio assistant Nava that he thought someone was going to die. Tim said to Nava, 'I hope it's not you.' And Nava replied, 'And I hope it's not you.'

Early the next morning Tim was woken by a dream. In the dream he was forced to the ground by a fierce beast like a wild dog, but it was more than a dog, it was a monster. As it came towards him he was wondering how he could defend himself, but the animal was so fast and so ferocious that he gave up hope. 'I was shocked by that dream,' he said. 'I had the feeling I had miscalculated, and that I was face to face with something I hadn't thought possible, the feeling of being powerless and of having to accept something that suddenly became inevitable. That,' he said, looking at me, 'was what happened to Nick.'

•

A couple of weeks before Nick's death, he had asked Tony and Ester, our cleaners for many years, to clear out some old rubbish and mouldy books from his storage unit to make way for Nick's papers from his office. Tony said to his wife, 'Why are we doing this now before he's dead?'

'You thought that because you were throwing out his old things?' I said to Tony.

'No, I clean out people's stuff from their houses and storage all the time, and I never had that bad feeling. But when I have bad feelings I know it means something.' Tony had been born in a small village in Nigeria and as a child had been privy to acts of black magic. He remembers seeing a poison being made in his father's home that cut a dog in half. 'I have seen many things; I know when members of my family or friends back home are sick or dying.' He said, 'But we can't stop these things from happening. It is God's will.'

•

Last night I had a dream. I was covered in bee stings: the stingers were all over my body; they had penetrated deep into my skin. I looked at a woman with an expressionless face who could not see me, and I said, 'I must get to a hospital.'

'Why?' said the woman uninterestedly.

'I have to get these things out of my body. I know I have to.'

'Oh, you'll be right,' she said.

•

I had another dream. I was with a group of people in a dark room with Nick's coffin and we were waiting our turn to see him. Antony was there too; he was dressed in blue velvet trousers and a black shirt. He was thinner and had a mop of black hair. He gestured to me to come with him to look at Nick. I shook my head and refused to follow him. When he was gone I went up to the coffin and pulled back the sheet covering Nick's face. I was worried about what he might look like after all this time; it had been almost a year. His eyes were moving and his eyelashes were flickering and he said, 'I'm moving quite a lot, as you can see, and I'm very glad.' He did look happy.

•

For many years I was ill with an undiagnosed autoimmune disease. I was always exhausted. I forced myself through the days; putting on my shoes in the morning was an act of will, and walking on flat ground felt like walking up a steep hill.

On our first meeting in the coffee shop Nick asked me my age; when I told him he was taken aback and said he had thought I was many years older than I was. He was disappointed and worried that perhaps I was too young for him. I am glad I looked ten years older because otherwise he might not have invited me for that coffee. It took a few years before I found a homeopath who diagnosed me, and slowly and miraculously, over a period of a few years, I became well, and for the first time in my adult life I could run or walk or do anything I pleased without having to force myself. As the years passed, I found my youth. And, even more miraculously, I no longer felt driven by a cantankerous will, I could allow my desires to emerge. Almost daily I used to watch a very large Fijian man walk past our apartment. I liked the slow-moving way he walked down the street, one step at a time, as if he had all day. We never acknowledged one another. One day he stopped and spoke to me for the first time. He looked at me astonished. 'I just have to tell you, lady—you look years younger.'

Nick said that I was getting younger every year because I was with him. 'I've always needed to love someone who needs to be loved,' he told me. He had a lot of love to give. And he loved loving. Sometimes I can still feel his caramel-coloured eyes upon me as I dress in front of the mirror. He used to take such delight in watching me dress; knowing what suited me better than I did, he would often advise me what to wear. And he loved watching me take my clothes off. When I stepped into the shower he would look at me with adoration and say, 'Beautiful!'

At night, in our front room, the streetlight on the trees casts trembling shadows and when it is windy they dance mysteriously upon the white walls. And while the sighs from passing cars ran through our hearts like the wind, we loved among those green shadows, we loved gravely, and tenderly, within the inner recesses of our being, protecting one another's solitude, to the brutal discordant rhythms of Ástor Piazzolla, or the unyielding cries from Miles Davis's trumpet, evoking every emotion that has ever been felt by man or woman. Together our ardour was forever renewing itself, we were like an oak tree growing; the force of our love running through our roots and stems, and when we touched we felt it in each other's veins. While we were loving we were in a kind of state of ecstatic waiting.

In my homily I had said we were two heads and two hearts together. Our souls were joined at our feet. Rachel put it differently: 'When you met you both had an orgasm, with your minds.'

Marta looked into my face and said, 'I can see Nick in your eyes now.' She picked up a photograph of him and studied it. 'Yes. Your eyes are like his now.'

I said, 'I can feel him in my eyes too.'

We were two birds with wings, an eddy on a warm spring day, a ribbon curling upwards. That's how we made love. Every time. I must never forget our last words to one another. When he dropped me at the station that fateful morning, I got out of the car and said to him, 'I want to make love to you.'

'Me too,' he said.

•

Glenn Gould wrote that when he was thirteen he had an epiphany: he was playing a softer passage on the piano and because of the nearby vacuum cleaner he couldn't hear what he was playing—'I could imagine what I was doing, but I couldn't actually hear it.' That's when I realised that the artist must always re-evaluate what he has been taught against 'that vast background of immense possibility—the imagination'.

I have been deaf in one ear since I was a young child, and half deaf in the other ear. I could hear a pin drop in a quiet room but if there were two or more sounds, any background noise at all, I was suddenly profoundly deaf.

I had learnt to lip-read a little but also to imagine what people were saying. Missing every third word or so meant I had to fill in those gaps. My limitation was an instrument, it gave me the ability—to use the beautiful phrase from William Lynch, SJ—'to imagine the real'. I would have liked to hide within a fantasy world, but my impairment set me on a much better course; it drew me out of myself into reality. When Nick and I discussed the qualities that were most important for him as a curator, he mentioned 'the ability to alter perception' and 'the need for uncertainty'.

Nick asked me what the most important thing for me as an artist was. Without hesitating, I said, 'Imagination.' But not fantasy. Fantasy shuts the door on life. If I turn my back on reality I know I must return to it at any cost. Steve put it well: 'Art does ask that we be able to enter into the world of another. But not to enter it with rape and pillage, rather to enter with love. That requires imagination. People often think of imagination as sitting in a tree, thinking up various fantasies, of wonderlands. But it's not just that. To imagine is to be able to appreciate what others are going through, to enter into their experience.'

I used to have to hold Nick's hand at the dentist when he had his teeth cleaned, when he was given an injection. How could it be that someone who was so scared of a needle was stabbed seven times? Nick was brave enough to enter a dark stairwell in Paris armed with a Le Creuset frying pan to ensure that it was safe for me, because a strange man had been bothering me at the door. He stood his ground when he was attacked by a dog on a lonely bush track. Maybe he was so frightened of his son that he couldn't ask for help. Perhaps he didn't have the imagination to see his son as a violent man?

•

I thought about Xu Wang in our sunny kitchen; he was making a preparatory drawing of Nick for a portrait for the Archibald Prize.

I stood behind Xu and watched him work the page, looking up at Nick and down again at the image quickly forming on the paper.

'You work too hard,' he said to Nick as he outlined his face with charcoal. 'You even work while you're having your lunch. You're an old man now. Why not take some time and enjoy yourself a little?'

I watched Xu's pencil fill the shadows on Nick's face; he made them much darker than the shadows cast by the light from the window. He saw the deep ridge between Nick's brows and marked it on the paper, and put a fire in his eyes—something fierce that I could not see. It took someone from another part of the world to come into this room and see Nick's soul. When Xu was finished he showed it to us. Nick was pleased with it.

'You've captured Nick's passion,' I said. I didn't tell him that I thought it also depicted his torment and anger—a darkened soul.

Nick stood up for the things he believed in, and with his work he didn't compromise. When it came to choosing which path to take on our morning walk it was always Nick who made the decision. With his gentle affirmative manner he would convince me that his way was really the way I wanted to go. I'd point to the left. 'Wouldn't you rather go right?' he'd say. And I'd believe him, and even think it had been my idea. In his workplace this was how he got things done, and, of course, he didn't mind others taking credit for his ideas.

But when it came to dealing with his children or his mother, any conflict at all seemed to freeze him into an utterly passive state. It was as if he was suddenly caught staring blindly into the sun. He couldn't say no.

And he didn't have much luck diverting me from my purchase in a Paris department store. After scouring the racks I had made my decision. I held up a black T-shirt with one word on the front in simple white lettering: *Non*.

Nick examined it carefully and frowned. The shop assistant came up to us, and seeing Nick's troubled face, she asked if everything was all right.

'*Ça va?*'

'*Oui, ça va, merci*,' I replied firmly.

The assistant looked at Nick, who was now looking really quite perturbed. '*Ça va?*'

'*Oui*,' I said again.

'You really think you will wear this?' Nick said.

'Yes.'

I thought to myself how I needed to say this word. And more than say it. I needed to *wear* it.

'This T-shirt has been made for me,' I said.

I needed to say '*non*' to indifference, '*non*' to lack of empathy, '*non*' to selfishness, '*non*' to pride, '*non*' to humiliation, '*non*' to glibness, '*non*' to fear, '*non*' to cowardice, '*non*' to lack of commitment, '*non*' to ingratitude, '*non*' to envy, '*non*' to entitlement, '*non*' to resentment; '*non, non, non, non, non*'. A thousand times '*non*'.

By now Nick was looking almost sick with anxiety. It irritated me. 'He chooses his T-shirts and he doesn't ask my permission,' I thought. 'And some have statements on them.' His favourite T-shirt bore the words: *Work in progress*.

'Don't worry,' I said, trying to lighten the mood. 'I'm not asking for your approval. I'm just showing you what I'm going to buy.'

I bought the T-shirt, and wore it. I showed it to the world as we strolled down the sunny rue de Seine on our way to lunch.

It didn't stop the thief from stealing my handbag, which was hanging on the back of the chair in the cafe, and walking out with it under his jacket. That afternoon I lost all my valuables: my writing, passport, money and bank cards, my camera, dozens of poems, and four years worth of photographs, which I'd never got around to downloading.

We spent the rest of that afternoon in the consulate applying for a new passport. That thief taught me a lesson. Wearing the word '*non*' is not enough.

•

One night I told Jane, 'I have often thought of joining him.'

'You could do that, but if you leave this world you won't be with him,' she warned.

When I told Steve, he said, 'Oh? There isn't anyone I would want to leave this life for.'

I placed my hand on the giant root of a fig tree above the ground. It felt the way Nick's hand did in the morgue. 'He reached out his hand to touch the laurel trunk. Under the rough bark he could feel her heart throbbing.' I repeated the masterful lines by Ovid.

'I am honoured to feel so much pain,' I said.

'That's a good way of putting it,' Steve said.

•

I used to drop eleven-year-old George off at school, and as he scrambled out of the car I would call out: 'You wouldn't be here if it wasn't for the work of so many others who came before you. You would be dead already from that school sore, your infected leg, or scarlet fever.' He would put his fingers in his ears.

I would not be here now if it wasn't for the *Lady and the Unicorn* tapestries, for Lucian Freud, Montaigne, Filippo Lippi, Leonardo da Vinci and Hieronymus Bosche, Goya, Rembrandt and a thousand other artists, and Nick.

•

Only a few days before Nick died, we went to see the Woody Allen film *Whatever Works*. In the cinema Nick reminded me to turn off my mobile.

'There's no need,' I told him. 'You're the only person who calls me.'

A woman sitting behind us laughed.

PART FIVE

The continuing gift

I can look at a beautiful landscape but I can't carry it with me. I can photograph it but that can only convey one view at one particular moment, whereas a painting can capture a particular place and time that can also be for all time, can be returned to time after time after time. In that sense a painting is more useful to me than the memory of witnessing a landscape, a sunrise or sunset or cascading waterfall or gently undulating river, each in their changing light. For example, to be surrounded by Monet's waterlilies at the Jeu de Paume in Paris is infinitely more rewarding than visiting Giverny.

From Nick's notebook

It was a cold, dry winter's day when Nick and I walked into Central Park and across to the Wollman Rink. We leant on the railing and watched the upright figures gliding over the rink as though being pulled along by an invisible magnet under the ice. We stopped at the edge of a pond, all seal grey and covered with a film like a thin layer of plastic. We looked into its depths and, with childish delight, saw a few bright red autumn leaves and someone's toothbrush caught in the ice.

We walked through the rusty-coloured grounds of Cedar Hill along a curved pathway lined with green wooden benches. Each bench bore a small brass plaque with an inscription. 'To the park lovers,' read one. Another read, 'Remember our happy days watching the dogs.' 'Happy tenth birthday, Wenke.' 'For Lily, on her ninetieth birthday.' And there was one that was more direct: 'Your husband loves you.'

We talked for a few minutes about the dead. How did Wenke celebrate his birthday? I saw the kind face of 'your husband' standing in a queue in a deli. And there was Lily, sitting on one of these benches, wrapped in a grey coat, leaning on her stick, and looking up at the cedars in new leaf. I wondered what she was thinking.

I recalled a passage from a hymn: 'How still and peaceful is the grave! Where, life's vain tumults past . . . The wicked there from troubling cease, their passions rage no more; And there the weary pilgrim rests from all the toils he bore.'

Through the chestnut trees the stone wall of the Metropolitan Museum suddenly appeared. 'Let's go,' said Nick. We climbed the steps and entered the Great Hall. We thought the museum was open that night but we were told that it would be closing in one hour. One hour at the Met. We were leaving the next day. 'To the American wing.' I took his hand and he led me to a work by Arthur Dove. I paused before the title, one of the most beautiful: *Reaching*

Waves. Waves like silver wings caught in flight—reaching for the shore. Then to Winslow Homer. Homer pushes these seascapes into one's heart; it's impossible not to feel in awe of the raging sea, to smell the salt and the fear. We raced through the galleries and stopped at *The Harvesters* by Bruegel. Nick didn't talk much when we were in front of a work. He moved off and I followed him.

What now? I was almost running behind Nick. We came across it while rushing through a room. 'There it is,' said Nick. In a gilt frame there was an old man with doubts, ready to face uncertainty. His soft eyes were searching, inwardly—outwardly. Dressed in brown, wearing the colour of his background, he was integrated into his world. Under his large black velvet cap, his querulous face was worn and tired but he was upright, robust, undefeated. Candid and self-effacing, he revealed a heightened consciousness of self that was reassuring and immensely touching. This was the Rembrandt that had been bequeathed to the museum in 1913 by Benjamin Altman. The other portraits in the room were of people who had lived and died long ago. By contrast, this self-portrait was of a man who, although not that far off death, was very much alive. With a slightly resigned look, and an acceptance of his place in the world, and of his fate, his life was unfolding behind him and there was a foretaste of what was to come. We thought we could read his thoughts and feelings in the shadows of his face. Rembrandt had captured a moment, a moment for all time. We could have stood in front of that painting for days, but we tore ourselves away. Nick looked at his watch. Only fifteen minutes to go. To *The Virgin Annunciate* by Antonello de Messina, another sacred and timeless icon. Her face was framed by the heart-shaped opening of her soft blue shroud. She was so still that I could feel myself shaking. Her hand, open and reaching out, was foreshortened in such a manner that she appeared to be physically touching something invisible that was outside the canvas. Her gaze, always beyond the viewer, made it impossible not to feel as if one was in the presence of another in the room; this other, according to the literature, was supposedly the archangel Gabriel.

We went to the European section where a guard warned us that the gallery would be closing in three minutes. That was enough time to fly through the rooms that were hung with Monet and Van Gogh. Such joy and air and light! Another guard was standing in the corner; her pulled-back hair severely tightened her face. Her eyes held onto us like a steel clamp as we walked quickly around the room. She was willing us to leave. We joined the throngs on their way out, passing through a subtly lit gallery where drawings from the permanent collection were on display. Nick stopped me to look at a small work by Van Gogh; its tiny ink markings capturing the wind, so much movement felt in such a few short strokes. Something drew me to one small drawing on the far side of the room. It was by Daumier and it depicted an old man sitting under a tree. The words under the picture told me that Van Gogh had also set his eyes upon this drawing, and he had written about it in a letter to his brother Theo, telling him that this work showed him how worthwhile it was to paint such a simple and ordinary subject. The last drawing we saw was in pen and ink by Ribot, a portrayal of a war casualty. Unlike so many others I had seen whose violent deaths were depicted in torment, this was the figure of a woman lying serenely on her back. Her body, still supple, was sensuously draped over the ground where she had fallen; it conformed to the undulations of the mountain range in the distance, hills that had been moulded so long before and would continue regardless.

I thought about those empty park benches and their dedications, the rooms in that great museum, and then the paintings and drawings themselves—those wondrous gifts of life. We flew down the steps and into the Great Hall. Four giant urns stood in their recesses, and there was another, larger urn in the centre; they were filled with tall sprays of pink quince blossom. We hadn't noticed them on the way in. Were they real? I had to find out so I went up and touched one of the tiny petals. Yes. They were. A plaque below the urn read: 'These fresh flowers are the continuing gift of Lila Acheson Wallace.'

A sharp pain rose from deep within and hardened my chest. My throat ached. I saw four tall men in coats walking towards me and I quickly turned so they would not see my eyes that were now filling with water. Nick noticed and he squeezed my hand tight. We understood each other without needing to say a word. While he went to collect our coats and the crowd began to clear, I stood for a few moments, thinking. What was this? Was it the notion that these flowers would always be fresh, that this gift was ongoing, forever renewing? Was it the sight of blossom in mid-winter—blossom which has the ability to contract time to one fleeting and transient moment? In one micro-second those tiny pink petals seemed to encapture the essence of all I had seen and felt that afternoon; here, in a moment condensed, was the mystery of life perpetuating itself for ever and ever.

We were among the last to leave. We put on our coats, and as we walked out the main door we looked back and saw the guards forming a circle around the information desk. In the centre, high on its pedestal, was the giant urn of pink blossom. Perhaps this was a ritual to mark the end of the day, a gesture of comradeship, a time to commune, for these workers who spend their days in a room alone. It was a curious sight, an image at once funereal and celebratory. Dressed in black, the men and women were standing very still and not speaking. It was probably just my fancy, but for a moment it seemed to me as if they were standing in silence for those quince blossoms. Then suddenly the circle broke and the guards dispersed in different directions, and Nick and I walked down the steps into the darkening street, sharing our silence.

Nick's passion

Ars longer, vita brevis: art is long, life is short.

As a curator, Nick's measure was his passion—all he needed was four walls. Nick was planning an exhibition which he never realised; it was to be called *The Exquisite Corpse*. It was inspired by research on a book he was writing: how Australia presented itself to the world and how the world embraced Australian art since 1961 through exhibitions. He wanted to collaborate with a few terrific curators he had a lot of time for, whom he believed in: each curator would choose one artist and one work, without knowing what the next curator would choose or what the previous had chosen. Nick explained:

> The title came from the Surrealist game of an artist drawing something, folding the paper, and passing it on to the next artist, who does not know what his predecessor has done; so when you open it up, you've

got ten different aspects in one form, but there's a coherence because it's all on one sheet of paper. It would encompass a particular view of the artist, side by side against another artist, and show two views, three views, a variety of views of the world at the one time.

The collaborators Nick felt close to were Hetti Perkins, Djon Mundine, Ross Mellick, Leon Paroissien, Bernice Murphy. He told me he felt spiritually and curatorially very close to Harald Szeemann, and he admired people like Seth Siegelaub, the first of the independent curators, and Nick Serota. 'They are all special: all visionary, courageous, and prepared to go against the grain and follow their beliefs.'

Nick was also interested in a sequel to *Spirit and Place*, the exhibition he created with his dear colleagues Ross Mellick, Hetti Perkins and Djon Mundine. 'A lot of people would want that to happen: a lot of people wanted it to be on permanent exhibition.' *Spirit and Place* was a conversation spanning a one-hundred-year period that brought together both Indigenous and non-Indigenous, and gave others a deeper understanding of the nature of their own relationship with the land and their spirituality. 'It talked about the spirit of this country in a way that no other exhibition has. Many people saw for the first time the complexity and richness of Indigenous art and the way non-Indigenous artists also responded with such sensitivity to this land and its psyche and its spirit.' Nick thought art could add greatly to the sharing of a spiritual understanding. For him all was intertwined.

•

Nick curated three Sydney Biennales, the first in 1979. *European Dialogue* created a dialogue between Australian contemporary artists and European artists. It was an historic event for it was the first time Aboriginal artists from Arnhem Land were included in an important international Biennale; it was a pivotal starting point for Aboriginal art to enter into the dominant Australian consciousness.

Nick's 1986 Biennale, *Origins, Originality and Beyond*, questioned the role of originality in art and in post-modernism and how it affected Australian contemporary artists. It had a subtitle: Was post-modernism the death or a resurrection of originality? Nick was always supporting himself with quotations in order to express himself less abstractly and he quoted Herbert Read: 'Originality is not the urge to be different from others; it is to grasp the origin, the roots of both ourselves and things.' He cited Joseph Beuys, who had died that year, as the visionary hope who underpinned the exhibition, bridging the gap between science and art, and again from Beuys: 'Only the human being, because he is free, can make the interconnections between the species. The human has the power to change, the free possibility to act today in the spirit of the wolf or fox, tomorrow who knows how?'

In his catalogue essay for the 1988 Biennale *From the Southern Cross*, Nick cited these lines from Alexander Solzhenitsyn:

It is useless to assert what one's heart does not believe. A work of art carries its proof in itself. Artificial, strained concepts do not withstand the image-test; all such concepts crumble, they are revealed as puny and colourless, they convince nobody. But works which have drawn on truth and presented it to us in live, concentrated form, grip us and communicate themselves to us compellingly—and nobody, even centuries later, will ever be able to refute them.

In this Biennale, Australian artists were placed side by side with their peers from Europe and America and New Zealand and Japan. Braque's late landscapes were placed alongside Fred Williams, Viola and Kiefer with Peter Booth, Balthus, Bill Fontana, David Smith, Gascoigne, Parr, Rothko, Hilton, Bonnard, Preston, Nolan, Lye, Deacon, McCahon and many other extraordinary artists from 1940 to the present. For Nick the single most important statement in the 1988 Biennale was the inclusion of the Aboriginal memorial of two hundred hollow log bone coffins, one for each of the two hundred years of white settlement. As Djon Mundine wrote: 'The burial poles from Ramingining were commissioned to represent two hundred years of white contact and black agony.'

All three Biennales revealed an approach that was suspicious of the stereotypical, allowed room for scepticism, resisted paraphrase, posed questions, and above all, offered to others the experience that Nick valued most one of change—and changing often.

•

Nick worked for a small art college gallery because he never wanted to conform to the sort of program a large institution inflicts on a curator. 'I've never been interested in wielding extreme power, making or breaking an artist's career,' he said:

> I've chosen to not continually be in the limelight because I think that would necessitate a frontal ego where one is constantly being asked, as a museum director, your opinion about everything, from the colour of socks to the worth of Tim Storrier's work or the Archibald Prize and everything else in between, which is not the way I like to work. I like to actually maintain separation between my public persona and my private persona. I've always been interested, as Duchamp used to try to do, to challenge my own beliefs—to surprise myself. I preferred to create a few 'poems in space' but I didn't think up that delightful phrase from Harald Szeemann.

'I'm at my best when I feel not absolutely at home,' he said. 'I'm an outsider. It gives me a double view because it enables me to distance myself slightly and yet be close to the people who live here.' Nick knew loneliness as a child and he was private; he thought perhaps he kept too much to himself but that meant he was always looking for conversations with himself, and that was how he became attracted to art:

> I tried to go through a process of ridding myself of every preconception as it appeared, and gradually, cloud after cloud, the clouds disappeared until there was blue sky, and I was actually looking at, say, what Pollock made, rather than thinking about what he's done, and it was

an absolute revelation because suddenly the energy of that work entered my body.

Nick knew that art can be slow to reveal itself—that it waits to be seen. He approached art the way a poet approaches a subject, without imposing himself on it. He also approached exhibition-making in the same way—pondering, choosing:

> The artist, it goes without saying, is the monarch, but the curator or exhibition-maker exercises the crucial choice of which artist and which work. We are what we choose, and in that sense the act of choosing is much more important than most people think. And that's what the curator has to do.

Nick was drawn to artists who could lay themselves bare, and to the work that exposed their deepest desires and fears, and he believed that pain was an artist's greatest resource. I can still hear his words: 'You need to go deeper into your pain, Juliet.' But it wasn't only the artworks that Nick wanted to respond to. As a curator and as a member of the community, Nick felt he had a responsibility to listen to artists and to respond intelligently to them. To be *with* them, to commune with them. When I spoke at Nick's memorial at COFA, a few months after his death, the words I was most proud of saying were: 'Nick could help artists because he loved them.'

When Nick first arrived in Australia from England in 1965 he saw that distant points could be eternally linked, such as the ancient Mimi figures of Aboriginal art and the prehistoric remains found in the caves of northern Spain:

I think essentially you can't possibly separate contemporary art, which so many people do, from the past. I think the art of the past is alive in any era. For me artists like Titian, Rembrandt and Vermeer, Piero della Francesca, just to name four, their work is as fresh now as it was when it was painted, so I see absolutely no separation between remarkable art of any era that transcends its moment and is timeless.

In his homily, John Wolseley told the congregation about a book, *The Star Thrower* by Loren Eiseley, with an introduction by W.H. Auden. In it Auden remarks how we humans are the only animal that works, prays and laughs. And how when we truly laugh we laugh simultaneously *with* and *at*. He wrote: 'Laughter is at the same time a protest and an acceptance.' 'Nick's laugh was like that,' said John. 'There was that quicksilver quality of change from great hilarity to a look of gravity. "Ah, that's what is serious," he might imply.' Nick took everything seriously, which I think was why he could find the ridiculous in everything and why he could delight in whatever exists. John went on to tell us:

Auden's three qualities, work, laughter and prayer, were all so strongly present in Nick. By 'prayer' Auden wrote that he did not mean 'the petitioning aspect of prayer, prayer at its most trivial—but the habit of listening'. A profound and intense receptiveness reminds me of Simone Weil and how she wrote: 'Love for our neighbour being made of creative attention is analogous to genius.' How beautifully that phrase 'creative attention' describes Nick and what a creative listener he was!

When Nick looked at art it did seem that he was listening with his eyes. Sometimes he would stand and look at a work for a long time. I asked him if he ever prayed. 'I have prayed when I have looked at works of art,' he said, 'but it's not something I insist on doing.' He told me about the day before his first partner died. Ross Mellick was with him in the hospital, and he saw that Nick was very distressed and asked him if he would like to have a swim or go for a walk in the park. Nick said, 'No. I want to see Rosalie Gascoigne's exhibition at the Art Gallery of New South Wales.' He told me, 'I went there on my own and I just was somehow able to think through the whole process of this person with whom I'd shared so much of my life, about to depart forever—and the work, and the thinking behind the work of Gascoigne gave me the strength somehow to continue and face what had to be faced. I prayed for her soul in front of the work, it seemed the most natural thing to do.'

Nick was a young boy when he was first moved by a painting. It was a work by Pieter Bruegel. He told me: 'I could happily expire in a room at the Kunsthistorisches Museum in Vienna where there are several extraordinary Bruegels—probably the painting of children playing games or that wonderful painting of winter. Somehow those wonderfully joyous paintings encapsulate, in the most enchanting way, all the things that I'd been moved by.'

One of Nick's great privileges, as a curator, was being able to work with extraordinary Aboriginal and Torres

Strait Islander art and artists. In my speech at the COFA memorial I said that it saddened me to think that he never fulfilled his wish to visit their country. After the memorial I received an email from Steve saying, *He is out there, in that country now.*

A Curator's Last Will
and Testament

1. Passion
2. An eye for discernment
3. An empty vessel
4. An ability to be uncertain
5. Belief in the necessity of art and artists
6. A medium—bringing a passionate and informed understanding of works of art to an audience in ways that will stimulate, inspire, question
7. Making possible the altering of perception.

When Steve suggested that the qualities in Nick's curator's will were not solely for curators, his words had resonance. Nick always drew himself to others, as he did to a work of art. His soft, focused caramel eyes would glow with delight and surprise whenever he met a person; with openness and tireless curiosity, he brought an intensity and his entire attention to every meeting, giving the other person the sense I always had when we reunited that he and I were meeting for the first time. Beginning again. Steve's words were the inspiration to make a film for Nick.

We had filmed Nick's funeral and I wanted to include the rites and Steve's poetic homily. I thought, 'Oh, people have to see this!' But I realised, in hindsight, it was actually me who wanted to see it, again and again, because I just couldn't stop thinking about it and I still couldn't believe it. And in the process of assembling the film we painfully watched Steve performing the rites with water and incense again and again. But I think it was a helpful thing for me to do, if bizarre.

Steve, who has such a passionate nature himself, spoke about passion:

> It is interesting that the first thing Nick wrote [about in his curator's will] was the word 'passion'. It comes from the Latin *patio*, which means to suffer, and even the word 'suffering' means 'to bear, to hold'. With a work of art or with art in general, it touches on all those places in life where there is pain, where there is suffering, where things have been broken open. Nick had the ability to engage at that level with pain in a work and other people's pain . . . [he] was prepared to stand there and be open to it. There's a Greek word, *splangthon*—'his whole guts come out'. And I think Nick's saying, 'Let your guts pour out, let your guts respond at that level to the work.'

Nick was religious, and Steve gave great insight into Nick as he made connections between passion and prayer, and prayer and looking at art:

The only thing we bring to prayer is our passion, our great desire for the great mystery. It may be . . . 'I want mercy, I want peace, I want whatever you can give me, the source of life. I want everything!' However you might say it. But if you don't want anything, well, nothing happens. You kind of wander in and wander out. But the desire, the passion—that's what you really want! So it's like a prayer, looking at a piece of work. And then . . . you just have to wait. Wait and receive.

I can just see Nick rocking on his heels, gazing, contemplating, allowing the work to reveal itself and wanting to bring that to others. Saying, 'Look, our world is never the same, we are never the same, at any moment.' We can all live that way with one another.

I interviewed John Wolseley, who offered to talk about 'an empty vessel':

The thing I remember about Nick, perhaps more than anything else, is his sense of sheer delight at certain things. He would . . . almost go kind of quivery with delight. And it was, I think, allied to the kind of delight which you have when you're walking with a six-year-old child, sometimes. It's a kind of primal delight which is, in a way, a kind of innocence, isn't it? But it's also a love of certain things. Nick had a quality which is rare even amongst artists or poets. A quality, which, as a curator, had a particular kind of magic to it. He had a wonderful ability to start from scratch each time. There was an awful lot of looking. Just . . . I'd say listening to what one was trying to do.

Nick's friend Ross spoke of the document: 'It's a very moving thing to do, isn't it? I wonder if he intended to elaborate on each of those points. Or whether they were just to remain there as windows for people to . . . open and explore imaginatively.'

Ross took us back in time to describe the way Nick understood contemporary art:

Nick knew, from the inside, that there was something about the art project that was truly dangerous. It was on the horizon. It's a mysterious thing, which is sort of on the edge, on the meniscus of human consciousness. That it was a reaching out towards some sorts of extremities. I think Nick also understood that the reaching out was not a straining towards something new or novel, but a straining towards something which was perhaps very old. And that the project of art was to identify and rediscover it, again, at each age.

•

I wanted to finish the film with these words from John Wolseley's homily at St Mary's:

Two weeks ago, I was standing on the edge of the huge flood plain of Garangalli in the wildest reaches of East Arnhem Land. I was with some very special artists and the great Yolngu artist, Djambawa Marawili, and his friend. As we looked out over the vast hazy plain with its mysterious clumps of trees and ancient middens, they were recounting the great ancestral histories of how in the 'first morning' two sisters came from the sea, and where they searched for food with their digging sticks, there are now freshwater springs. And how the first sun came up and they were turned into brolgas. As Djambawa was describing this, about fifty of those majestic birds appeared in the distance. With slow wing beats, they followed the vast flood plain in the direction from which the two sisters had come. I thought: How Nick would love this! Such a perfect alignment of spirit and place. And I leave you with this image of the flood plain and those birds—an image which reminds us of Nick's great respect for Aboriginal thought, and hints at the grand poetic reach and distant pathways of his wandering spirit.

Or as Hokusai wrote in his last days:

> Now as a spirit
> I shall roam
> The summer fields . . .

But the words and images from Nick's funeral raised more questions than I could or wanted to answer, such as: 'What was the story?' 'Who was Antony?' and 'Why did he murder his father and sister?' The film was getting further and further away from the open and questioning quality of Nick's 'Curator's Last Will and Testament'.

I showed the film to editor Roland Gallois, who asked me the most obvious question: why hadn't I included art in the film?

'Art? I can't do that, I can't afford to clear the rights,' I told him.

I had a choice to make. I could extend the film outwards, digress and make it philosophical, which would have been interesting to me but would take a lot more money and I would need a television sale; I had already sent the film to the ABC and to Screen Australia and they weren't interested. Or I could begin a process of simplification, make it an elegy—and include Nick's passion.

I had just finished tidying and filing the papers in Nick's office, a six-month job, and I had come across the thousands of postcards of artworks Nick had collected over a thirty-year period. Whenever he visited the art museums of the world he would make his way to the shop and purchase postcards. He never intended to send them; they were for his own reference. I often wondered what he was going to do with all those cards. I thought, 'Well, I have found something to do with them.' I had also come across a list, in Nick's handwriting, of the major works that had inspired him throughout his life. And on the list was a note to himself: *Just write about what you love, and forget the rest!* I used this list to select the artworks from his postcards. I spent rainy evenings among the shadows in our living room, continuing into the early hours of the morning, listening to every track on each CD from Nick's enormous jazz collection, something neither of us had had the time to do while we were together. I had everything I needed right here in our apartment. It was too simple. No wonder I hadn't thought of it.

Using the seven points in the curator's will as a guide, Roland and I grouped the artworks and then overlaid segments of music. The pieces were filled with creative tension, as were all the artworks themselves, and it had the magical effect of binding together those great, silent and disparate works. This was, after all, Nick's music.

'My Funny Valentine' by Miles Davis was recorded live at a benefit concert in 1964 for the registration of black voters in Louisiana and Mississippi. I read that Miles had decided to waive his fee, and also that his sidemen would do the same. But he hadn't thought to ask his musicians beforehand, and they didn't like the idea. Miles wouldn't change his mind, though.

'When we came out to play,' Miles wrote, 'everybody was madder than a motherfucker with each other and so I think that anger created a fire, a tension that got into everybody's playing, and maybe that's one of the reasons everybody played with such intensity. We just blew the top off that place that night. It was a motherfucker the way everybody played—and I mean everybody.'

'If I could have only one artist, it would be Goya,' Nick had told me many times. When I was a young woman in Paris I was shown, for the first time, Goya's *Los Caprichos* and I was so moved I began to weep. With the utmost relief, I thought, 'So, I can live in this world, after all.' I had had a protected childhood in the suburbs of Sydney, but when I saw those black-and-white etchings, depicting man's inhumanity to man—passions, weaknesses, failings, madness, persecutions, dreams, love and death—I seemed to recognise them as if I had already known them.

Roland and I began the film with works by Goya that would embody Nick's greatest passion. I downloaded a track initially just because of its title: 'Chelsea Bridge'. As a child Nick had lived in Chelsea, and his father, who died when Nick was three, and whose loss Nick always carried with him, must have seen the bridge at night too. The song, by Billy Strayhorn, was inspired by the Turner painting of

Battersea Bridge on a misty night—Billy had mistaken it for Chelsea Bridge. On our first trip to London, Nick had taken me especially to see both bridges. Roland placed this haunting tune, which seemed to draw pain out of the air, over the Goyas. We played the images with the music and looked at one another with astonishment. To use Miles's words, it was a motherfucker.

We grouped the remaining ninety-four artworks, ranging from Paul McCarthy, Joseph Beuys, Fiona Hall, Jagamarra, Mondrian, Wolfgang Laib to Maso di Banco, finishing with the rising screaming notes of Eddie Bronson's saxophone at St Mary's over Brancusi's *Column of Endless Delight*.

•

I saw that Steve's words were not only the inspiration for the film; they were the meaning, the poetry in the film. We filmed a number of takes of his speech; many were perfectly delivered but Roland and I chose the one where Steve paused to find his words. It was his struggle that moved us because he searched for the words in his heart:

Nick was talking about a piece of work, looking at it in a contemplative way, holding it from a point of view of being uncertain, bringing to bear all his capacity to sieve and sort through and discern. And we can relate to one another as Nick related to a piece of art; open to one another, without prejudgments, as an empty vessel and discerning with one another. And passionate—really engaging with the other, really wanting to hold that person, to suffer with that person, to be with that person. What he's saying about art—he's left that for us, to be that way with one another.

Nick had bequeathed to curators his most precious possessions. Pathetically, he had used the terminology of a legal document, but unlike property in legal wills, his possessions were not material. They were not a set of beliefs; they were the qualities Nick needed as a curator: to make connections with people, with art. In the film we included Nick's words: 'Ideas only flourish when they find connections. Connectedness equals love.'

•

When George was six I used to take him to the supermarket where a dwarf stacked the shelves; the man used to give the children a hard time in return for the long stares they gave him. For months, each time we drove down the main street past the supermarket, George would ask me: 'Mummy, will I grow?' I knew he was thinking about the dwarf.

'Yes,' I said.

'Are you sure?'

'Yes.'

'But how do you know?'

'I just know.'

When I was a child not much older than George then, I was preoccupied with a different question: whether or not I could love or would ever be able to love. At a young age I was thinking of death and love. We forget that children do think about these things.

An artist has to find love. Somehow they have to find humility in order to receive love, and then return it in the form of a work of art. I think this is what Lucian Freud meant when he said, 'The artist is nothing. The work is everything.'

•

Shelley wrote: 'Poetry lifts the veil from the hidden beauty of the world, and makes familiar objects be as if they were not familiar.' Poetry does that and death does it too.

The world, and all in it, is both familiar and no longer recognisable. I have seen it all before but I am seeing it all again—for the first time.

Death has erased the 'shoulds' and 'oughts', the 'what ifs' and 'coulds' from my vocabulary. Things are as they are. There are no 'whys' any longer—just 'whats' and 'so whats'.

I can hear the soprano next door singing the aria from *The Fairy Queen* and I see Braque's eternal birds in flight and think of Blake's words:

How do you know but ev'ry bird that cuts the airy
way Is an immense world of delight, clos'd by your
senses five?

Each day I go to the courtyard of the Hôtel de Sully to sit under the four-hundred-year-old holm oak. I make my way to the Jardin des Plantes and the three-million-year-old fossil of a sequoia tree, and I pass the curling browned petals of the irises that only a week ago were bright and violet and full of wonder.

I am still using the yearly pocket diary Nick gave me last Christmas. I turn the empty blue pages. These were the days we had planned to be together. They are not empty pages but days filled with pain. They will go on. The hours, the minutes on my watch don't belong to me any more than the stars above.

The red-and-white emergency tape crisscrossing the car park shudders in the wind: five white vans are parked near the leafy wall. The top branch of a linden tree rears up and falls like a horse. The world used to chatter, it used to speak to me, but now even the wind makes no noise.

•

Walking along the beach I saw a tiny white feather, as small as a goose feather, on the sand. A retreating wave picked it up and carried it out, and as I watched it floating on the foaming crest of the wave I thought of Nick's soul. I had read somewhere that the Egyptian goddess Maat used a feather to weigh the dead souls to determine whether they would reach the paradise of afterlife successfully.

•

Nick and I had been to an exhibition at a gallery in Sydney. In one corner was a hyperrealistic sculpture by artist Ron Mueck. In minute detail it depicted every hair and pore and sagging fold of flesh of the corpse of his father. Nick wouldn't look at it.

The sculpture was reduced in scale to about a third of its natural size. It was haunting. Its diminution is what death does. Death reduces the size of the world by exactly one-third.

At one of our soirées Nick told me to ask Eddie if he could play 'Non, je ne regrette rien'.

'That song! Oy. Whenever I play that song I think of all the things I do regret,' said Eddie.

The only family photo Nick kept on display on his dresser was a small framed black-and-white photo of his father wearing a suit; he was sitting on the ground with his hand outstretched. Nick had inherited the same serious half-smile and the same intelligent focused eyes. That was the one thing Nick regretted—never getting to know his father.

Under his beach house Nick had kept all his father's belongings: jazz records, personal effects from the war, a little fold-up record player for use on the battlefield. His father survived the Second World War but died soon after when he rolled his car in a country laneway. In 2007 we went to see a show of modern British painting at the National Gallery of Victoria. Nick stopped in front of a painting where a laneway meandered through summer fields enclosed by hedges. His eyes filled with tears. He told me that this picturesque setting reminded him of his father.

Recently I have seen those beautiful serene faces between earth and sky by Raphael, and miniature figures walking on waves on the wildest oceans on Tao scrolls. Matisse reds, and delicious purple and gold shadows in Bonnard. I saw the archetypal hieratic Maso di Banco *Madonna and Child*. In the Madonna's sombre open face was a detachment as if she was behind glass, her dark eyes looked straight through me to eternity.

Many times I was directed across the Seine to the Musée de Cluny to stand in front of the softly illuminated *Lady and the Unicorn* tapestries to be enchanted by her sadness, to be reminded that pain comes with wonder and delight.

That young woman estranged on that blue floating island was connected to something quiet and deep within. And she has raised so many questions that the centuries have not been able to answer.

I went to see Monet's ever-changing waterlilies, and Goyas, El Grecos, Breugels. But the putty-coloured bodies, plain naked faces and blood-engorged genitalia of the Lucian Freuds at the Pompidou spoke to me most loudly. The way those undressed figures were posed made it feel as if they might have been wearing clothes, and that made it seem that they were laying themselves bare. There was such hard concentration, a searching that went under the surface of things. In them I found the deep humility of an artist unconscious of himself. Grappling with ambiguities and tensions, they defeated indifference. Freud had said, 'Art is a way back to reality.' His works were a movement into life, a movement into the world. Open in hope, those paintings yielded secrets kept from the cynical. They seemed to capture the end of a moment, the death of a moment, just before one turns away or closes one's eyes. They were a balm to my soul and involuntarily I kept returning to them. A film with the poetic title *The God of Small Things* accompanied the exhibition, and these lines from it came back to me as I walked the streets: 'And when the last stars have extinguished there will be nothing left to say and it will still be more beautiful.'

Loss is no longer an illusion. I have been shunted backwards as if I am looking through the wrong end of a telescope, into the shadows of death. Death, now so close to me, has made me old enough, or should I say young enough, to be able to step outside of myself, and to look at the world and gasp with wonder.

Nick found the world through art. For him, art wasn't a substitute for life, it wasn't an escape from reality—it was a way into it. Perhaps it is the same thing: when I look at the world now I see a strange and livid beauty. I see life as a work of art.

The crime-scene photos: the sleep and peace of love

The Thomas Hirschhorn work in the Swiss Pavilion at the 2011 Venice Biennale resembled a weird cave from a science-fiction set, and a cheap disco: an assembly of crystals, shards of broken glass, images on television screens of violent deaths among everyday household objects, and many strange forms wrapped in silver foil. There was too much to take in; it was beyond one's grasp. It gave me an emotional orientation to a world that would always outstrip my experience. Nick and I had seen Hirschhorn's work in a commercial gallery in the Meatpacking District in New York. Nick was fascinated, and he gazed at the work, on the screens, at the blood, at the bodies torn apart lying sprawled—forgotten corpses on roadways. I took one quick look and walked back out into the street to wait for him.

But now I found that I could look at Hirschhorn's work. And that I needed to see it. The artist wrote: 'I want to cut a window, a door, an opening or simply a hole, into reality. I want to create a truth that resists facts, opinions and commentaries. I am not afraid of contradiction, conflict, resistance or complexity.'

It sort of reminded me of my experience when I first stepped into Steve's whole world of an office: in it there was room for everything—love and beauty and death, and, in the faces in the photographs of the street people, all the pain.

I thought to myself, 'If Nick could look at Hirschhorn's work then surely I can look at it all. I must look.' Nick would often say, 'The trouble with Australia is there is no theory of relativity.' He thought Australians didn't see things in context, they didn't want to look at the whole. That is why he would have wanted me to see the crime-scene photographs, to see the images of his death.

As I walked out of the Swiss Pavilion I ran into Rachel, and I told her then that I wanted to see the crime-scene photos. She looked at me sadly and said, 'Don't. Nick would much rather you see a Giotto fresco.'

I couldn't reconcile Nick's death with the image I had of him in the morgue. I was a little concerned about the effects of doing such a thing because for six months, each morning and each night, I used to wake and look for Nick in the green blanket, and replay the final moments of two lives. Every time the re-enactment was the same. I see Antony rummaging about in the kitchen drawers. Chloe isn't watching him. She is busy making tea. Then they argue. She doesn't notice Antony taking the knife from the drawer. Before she has time to realise what he is doing, Nick is struggling with Antony as they move down the corridor towards the front door. I see every muscle strained on Nick's face and I see the terror in Nick's eyes. Then I see the last thing Nick sees, Antony's demonic face, up close, the face of evil.

Why did I relive this horror? So I could brand it into my heart? After six months those scenes began to fade, but still I wanted to give the images that were isolated in my mind a perspective, and a place.

My doctor said, 'I don't recommend it. You're such a visual person.' My friend Sally said, 'Do it. I would want to if it was Paul.' The homicide detective said, 'I say no.' The counsellor at the morgue told me that the detective didn't want me to see them because he thought they would upset me. 'But it couldn't be worse than anything you have gone through,' she said.

In a shopping centre I bumped into a psychiatrist, a researcher on mental illness. I told him I was thinking of viewing the crime-scene photos. 'What do you think?' He told me he had seen some of his patients' autopsies as part of his work and said, 'I don't recommend it.' I looked up at him imploringly, 'Yes, but I loved him.'

As I walked away through the foodhall I thought, 'That's it. That makes it different. I think I can understand why the detectives and scientists, those who have to see these things as part of their job, wish to protect others from seeing them. But maybe they don't understand that when you love someone it is essential to look—at everything.'

I wrote a letter to the coroner and he gave me permission to view the photos. Steve offered to accompany me. He said he would hand me the photos. To look at the worst is no more than an active trust in God. It was appropriate that he was there to support me.

In the car on the way to the morgue I said to Steve, 'I need to deal with what has hurt me the most.'

Steve said, 'It was the women who wanted to be with Jesus when he died, and they were the ones who went to the tomb.'

The counsellor brought in the police file. She carefully described how the events of the evening unfolded, and explained to us in detail what we were about to see. We took the file to a desk by the window and the three of us sat down. One photo was a close-up of Nick's face. His eyes were open, unseeing. Another was a medium shot of his body, lying where he had fallen, slumped on one side in a sleeping position. A third showed his naked torso and the wounds on his chest. He was soaked in blood; he had been stabbed in the chest seven times, his stomach had been slashed. I put my fingers on his chest involuntarily; only afterwards was I aware that I had touched the photo, I had touched his wounds. The counsellor showed us three more photos, one was of Nick's watch on the ground. At lunchtime on the day he died, I had been to the Swatch shop in the city to buy him a replacement plastic band. There was a photo of Nick's wrist, which had been cut to the bone. Another showed the kitchen knife next to a ruler on a Persian carpet. It was the same knife I have in my kitchen, only bigger. 'He chose the biggest knife from those wooden blocks,' said Steve.

This is very strange, and these words cannot describe the experience, but looking at the images of horror, of violence, brought me peace. I saw that this murder had happened, and also that I wasn't there. Because I had replayed the events over and over, I had had the sensation that I had been at the scene of the crime. And if I had been there, why hadn't I done something to stop it? Why had I been merely an onlooker? When I saw the photos I understood for the first time that I wasn't there and I couldn't have stopped it. It was a frenzied attack. I saw the event in a new light and I felt the fire of my anger cooling. My anger had suddenly become a useless emotion. My opinions and judgments were irrelevant in the larger scheme of things. The reality of those images defied such conclusive thinking. I had distorted the events, magnified them and elevated them to the status of a dream which had more to do with myself than the actual events. My ideas and fantasies were contemptuous of reality and were more dangerous, more hurtful to me, than facing the stark facts of Nick's death. Death is the last moment—but it is just another moment. And then, I felt the sleep and peace of love.

That's what my friends and others couldn't understand. To look at it, to face it, that is what a lover has to do. That is what Nick had had to do with his son. Nick looked at death with his eyes open.

Nick died in the hallway by the front door; as he was facing his son who was brandishing a thirteen-inch knife, his wonderful last words, overheard by a neighbour, were: 'I love you.'

Acknowledgments

I thank my son George for his kindness and humility.

I would like to thank Jane Campion and David Malouf for encouraging me to write about my experiences. This memoir is the result. I thank my agent Brian Cook for his courage to support the book and for his faith, generosity and courtesy.

Many thanks to my friends Andrew Kotatko, Laura Jones, Jean Kent and Jane Campion for reading the manuscript and for their good counsel.

Many thanks to Rebecca Kaiser and Christa Munns at Allen & Unwin, and to my editors Ali Lavau and Clara Finlay, who all provided great help with this project.

Thanks to the Art Gallery of New South Wales who provided me with a residency at the Cité Internationale des Arts in Paris where much of this book was written. And thanks for the generous hospitality of the Cité Internationale des Arts.

I give special thanks to all those whose voices and actions make up this story, whose acts of kindliness and charity caught at my imagination and remain in my heart. This book was written with gratitude for you all.

I am especially grateful to Father Steve Sinn for his steadfast support and gentle thoughtful guidance during the aftermath of this tragedy, for his imaginative tact—all of which helped me to accept the suffering, which at times went far beyond what was bearable, and to realise that even the worst can be endured and has been given to us for an end.